BRITAIN IN OLD PHOTOGRAPHS

THE

MELTON MOWBRAY ALBUM

TREVOR HICKMAN

SUTTON PUBLISHING

Around Melton Mowbray first published by Alan Sutton Publishing Limited in 1992

Melton Mowbray first published by Alan Sutton Publishing Limited in 1993

This combined edition with corrections published by Sutton Publishing Limited in 1997

ISBN 0-7509-1699-0

Alan Sutton Publishing Limited is an imprint of Sutton Publishing Limited
Phoenix Mill, Thrupp, Stroud, Gloucestershire GL5 2BU

By the same author:
The Vale of Belvoir in Old Photographs
The History of Stilton Cheese
Around Rutland in Old Photographs
East of Leicester in Old Photographs

Cover photographs: front: Cheapside, Melton Mowbray, 1936; *back:* Bagrave End, Barsby, leading to Church Lane in 1906.

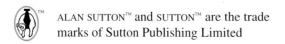
ALAN SUTTON™ and SUTTON™ are the trade
marks of Sutton Publishing Limited

Typeset in 9/10pt Sabon.
Typesetting and origination by
Sutton Publishing Limited.
Printed in Great Britain by
WBC Limited, Bridgend.

Part One
AROUND
MELTON MOWBRAY

Ploughing by Charles Simpson.

Plan of the parishes covered in this publication.

Contents

The Prince of Wales, Duke of Clarence with the Cottesmore Hunt, by Charles Simpson.

Introduction

When I am visiting various parts of England and discussion develops concerning my home town I find the immediate response is normally, 'Oh, that's where pork pies come from', or 'the centre for Stilton cheese' and sometimes, 'Yes! that's where fox-hunting commenced.' Most people living in this area of the country would agree with all three of these comments. What I have attempted to do in this book is to gather together old photographs that in some way depict our local interests, industry and what has happened over the last one hundred years in the Melton Mowbray district. It is my personal collection, for which I take full responsibility; there are glaring omissions throughout the book, often because I have not been able to locate a suitable photograph, and there are also restraints in producing a book such as this on how many photographs can be used.

During the early spring of 1992 I visited each parish listed on the plan on p. 4. In driving around this beautiful part of England with nothing better to do than look at the landscape and position ninety-year-old photographs into their present day setting, I noticed a number of features projected in sharp relief: the splendid panoramic variation of shades of green spreading before me; quaint stone-built villages nestling in the fold of a low sloping hill; the brown face of the stone cottages blending in with the lush green of the fields and trees. Out towards the Vale of Belvoir and the Lincolnshire flat lands strange brown cliffs of sandstone run along field headlands, a legacy of opencast ironstone mining in this part of Leicestershire. After Stilton cheese, pork pies and hunting, the production of iron ore was a major factor in providing employment for villagers in this area from the end of the nineteenth century to the 1950s. In my youth I was fascinated by the small gauge railway system operating on the edge of the Vale of Belvoir, and the drag lines with cabins that looked like half-timbered buildings and dotted the landscape around Buckminster and Sewstern. With the help of my late father-in-law and my miller friend from Soham Mill I have included photographs recording this chapter of the Industrial Revolution as it affected this area some thirty years ago. Some of the photographs are poor quality; because it was such an everyday occurrence to see opencast mining near your village very few people photographed the system. Even though the country-side was ripped apart, redevelopment of the land has been superbly carried out and in many instances it is very difficult to see where the mining took place as the hedges have been replanted, repeating the rectangular field system so important to the economy of this area.

As the sixteenth century enclosure awards began to take effect, and the large open fields were broken up into smaller hedged units, so farming methods changed. The lush grass meadows that gradually developed in the hawthorn-hedged enclosures witnessed the introduction of the herds of milking cows that produce excellent creamy milk so necessary to produce fine cheese. So cream cheese manufacture developed. It is presumed that some enterprising wife of a local farmer allowed some of her cream cheese to mature long beyond its normal 'shelf-life', thereby allowing the introduction of the grey-green mould so important in good prime Stilton. When and where did Stilton cheese originate? In my opinion it happened some time during the early part of the sixteenth century, almost certainly by accident. The earliest recorded account of its manufacture suggests it was made in a farm kitchen at Wymondham. There is hardly a village around Melton Mowbray that did not have a farmer making Stilton cheese, and most village historians state that it was made in their village first. Certainly it was made in very large quantities by the Pawletts of Wymondham at the end of the eighteenth century, and later by the Morris family of Scalford and Saxelby who certainly marketed the product in large quantities. Their cheese was sold in the village of Stilton on the Great North Road. A cream cheese, however, was being sold at The Bell Inn, Stilton long before the Pawletts were producing it. In the production of Stilton large surpluses of whey are created, which was mixed with recycled waste food and corn products to form 'swill', an excellent feed for pigs. Stilton cheese manufacturers normally farmed pigs, in sties adjacent to the dairy, for their bacon and ham which was salted down for subsequent use. On slaughtering the animals a considerable quantity of surplus pork was always available. This was used in pork pies, brawn and chitterlings among other products. There was hardly a cottage in this area of Leicestershire that did not fatten up a pig, the piglet having been purchased from the local dairy. Most kitchen shelves carried a whole range of wooden pork pie moulds. There was more than one farming unit incorporating a windmill where the miller provided the flour, the farmer's wife produced cheese, and adjacent pigsties provided pork for the pies that were baked on site in the large kitchen oven along with bread, all for general sale.

To provide good grazing land and to enclose the cows that produced such fine milk in this area, thick, well maintained hawthorn hedges are needed. On enclosing the large fields, small areas of wasteland were left. These developed into the spinneys that are dotted around the landscape, linking the field system together, and provided an ideal breeding ground for foxes. The spinneys provided the cover for the foxes' earths and the hedges provided an excellent system of covered trackways to allow this cunning animal access, under cover, to new hunting grounds. Having no natural enemies, the fox multiplied, and farmers had no choice but to hunt it down. The easiest method was with a pack of hounds, and so, as part of the necessary control of a pest that killed large quantities of poultry and young lambs, fox-hunting developed into a spectacular rural sport. Thus the landscape was maintained for centuries, supporting the farmers' needs and providing excellent jumps for the sporting fraternity with sufficient private funds who could indulge in this activity. The season was spent in Melton Mowbray, fine houses being built to meet the needs of the huntsmen. Hunting had many spin-offs: the sport provided considerable employment, and the locally produced cheese and pies were enjoyed by the huntsmen as well as the local population. Vast quantities were exported out of the area, and the manufacture of such products soon became a major industry in this part of the country.

Among this collection I have included photographs of people wherever possible, for without people we would have no record. After all, the part of the country in which we live is a man-made landscape. In a very short space of time, however, nature covers up the scars that we leave on the landscape by farming, industrial and military use. In my lifetime what were areas of dereliction have become listed sites of special scientific interest because of the wildlife that has returned – a fine example is Saltby Heath – and that is how it should be.

My collection is a pictorial record of this part of Leicestershire, and a contribution to the wealth of material already published, not a new idea. John Throsby, a local historian and artist, published his select views in 1789, and many other artists have done the same since that date, including Rigby Graham, who published his *Leicestershire* in 1980. Photography is a more accurate method but the artist often records features that the camera cannot see. That is why I have included a few photographs of various artists' impressions of the landscape in this book. All local history publications should be viewed together for what they are, bearing in mind that an individual or group will give its own interpretation of the features it has chosen to record. Not to be viewed in isolation, these publications present to the reading public a combined record of the countryside as the collectors see and observe it. This collection complements other publications of a similar type.

Some of the photographs used have never been published before and the major part of this collction is made up of photographs taken between the years 1900 and 1920, the golden age of photographic postcards. Very many of these photographs were sold as postcards, stamped with a halfpenny stamp, posted with the certain knowledge that it would arrive the next day. The messages written on the reverse are very interesting. Often they relate to the view on the face side and in some instances I have used this source material in compiling the captions in this book. Who were these early photographers? Many were employed by national and local agencies, and in this part of Leicestershire we had one outstanding photographer, W. Till, who worked on his own. Many of the early twentieth-century postcards reproduced here have his name on the face side. He travelled around the district on his bicycle, set up his plate camera on a tripod, selected the view, released the shutter and so recorded the scene. On returning to his studio in Melton Mowbray the glass plate was developed, and he then scratched his name and the title in reverse on the emulsion side of the plate and made one direct contact print. On returning to the location where the photograph was taken, days or even weeks later, he then attempted to sell further copies of the scene. In many instances he was not successful and only one print was made, thus explaining the rarity value of some early photographic postcards. Some of the views published in this book are reproductions of such scarce postcards. I trust the reader will enjoy them and that they will reach a wider audience than they were originally intended for.

This book is now reissued by popular demand as part one of *The Melton Mowbray Album* complementing *Melton Mowbray in Old Photographs*.

Section One
MELTON MOWBRAY

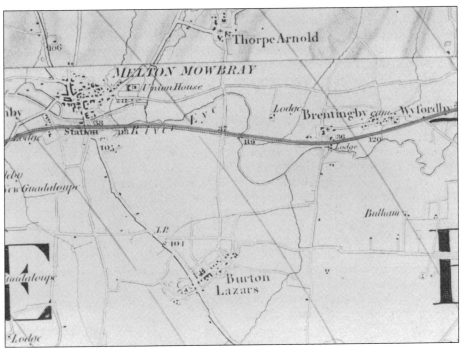

Section of the 1835 edition of the Ordance Survey, revised in 1867.

South Parade, *c.* 1900, showing J.W. Warner's lending library, printing and bookbinding establishment along with the stationery department and general bookshop on the left.

The White Hart public house on Thorpe End, *c.* 1908.

Melton Mowbray cattle market in 1907.

The Market Place in the centre of town in 1935.

Outside Leonard Gill's ironmongery shop in the 'Barnes Block' in 1908.

The cheese fair in the 1890s, with Stilton cheeses stacked on the cobbles in the Market Place prior to their being auctioned off.

The teaching staff of Melton Modern Boys School, Limes Avenue in 1952. Of the twenty-four people shown, twenty-one are identified, in alphabetical order: Messrs Anderson, Barnett, Bartlett, Berry, Cullen, Fox, J.V. Fox, Greaves, Greenslade, Greenway, Goode, Hirst, Jackson, Kaye, Mayo, Neal, Parrott, Rowell, Till, Timms, Troll.

A typical Melton Mowbray family group of the 1930s, posing outside No. 64 Salisbury Avenue in 1937. Back row, left to right: Judith Pulford, Fred Pulford, Jane Pulford, Louisa Burton, David Burton, Arthur Burton. Second row: Margaret Sansby, Alice Sansby, Jean Pulford, John Pulford.

The Northern railway station being demolished in 1967.

The Midland railway station in 1910.

Burton Street, showing the Boat Inn on the right, in 1900.

Burton Street Basin in the 1880s. The Boat Inn is on the right.

The 1936 Hospital Gala, showing the parade passing down Nottingham Street.

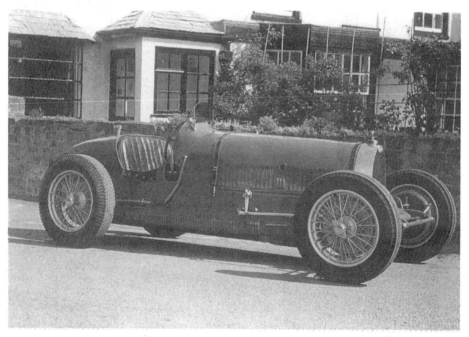

A 1930 straight eight supercharged Bugatti standing outside Toad Hall off Burton Street, near the Boat Inn.

Brook Street, November 1940. A lone German bomber strafed Sherard Street with machine-gun fire and dropped a bomb that landed in Scalford Brook between Regent Street and Brook Street killing one man and causing damage to surrounding properties.

Sherard Street and Thorpe End, flooded in August 1922. Compare this photograph with the one reproduced on p. 10.

The Limes, off Sherard Street, before the First World War. Woolworths store now stands on this site.

The Melton Breakfast photograph of an engraving by C.G. Lewis after a painting by Sir Francis Grant PRA. From left to right: Massey Stanley, Earl of Wilton, Count Matuscewitz, Lord Gardner, Walter Little Gilmour (in the armchair), Lyne Stephens, the club servant, Sir Frederick Johnstone (at breakfast), Lord Rokeby (reading a newspaper), Lord Forester (by the fireplace), Lord Kinnaird (writing), Rowland Errington, for whom the painting was commissioned in 1839. Above the fireplace is depicted a painting by John Ferneley. It is presumed this is a record of a breakfast at The New Club opposite The George on High Street prior to a day's hunting with the Quorn.

The Prince of Wales at Sysonby in 1925. The sporting prince, who became Edward VIII in 1936, made Melton Mowbray one of his retreats from his official round of royal duties.

Sysonby Lodge in 1911. In the early nineteenth century this was the home of Frederick Ponsonby, 3rd Earl of Bessborough, Baron Ponsonby of Sysonby, whose daughter, Lady Caroline Lamb, was passionately infatuated with Lord Byron. On seeing his cortege being transported along Nottingham Road, Melton Mowbray to Hucknall Torkard, she collapsed and her mind became unbalanced. She never completely recovered.

Thorpe Arnold toll-gate. In 1856 William Brown, alias Peppermint Billy, murdered the gatekeeper, Edward Woodcock, aged 70 and his 10-year-old grandson, James. For this crime Brown was hanged in front of Welford Road prison, the last public hanging in Leicester.

The base of the medieval market cross near the church of St Mary, Thorpe Arnold.

Section Two
THE WREAKE VALLEY AND
SETTLEMENTS TO THE NORTH

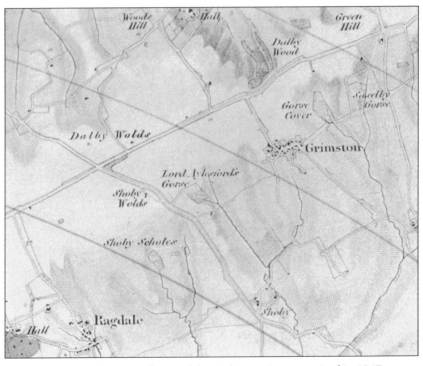

Section of the 1835 edition of the Ordnance Survey, revised in 1867.

A meet of the Quorn Hunt in 1906 at Kirby Gate, when Mrs Rippen was in residence.

The Cottage, 1925, home of John Brodie Esq.

Kirby Lodge, 1920. The Woodward family with their turkeys.

Kirby Lodge, 1921. Walter Woodward and Zillah Woodward with their children Laura, Bertha and Walter.

The Flying Childers public house in 1904, when John Walker was the licensee. The cottages shown are now a private house. The Childers is now a purpose-built public house further along the road. It was named after a racehorse owned by the 2nd Duke of Devonshire which, in 1719, was considered to be the finest racehorse in the world. A life-size portrait of the famous horse hangs in Chatsworth House, Derbyshire.

Main Street, Kirby Bellars, leading to the main Leicester road in 1916. To the right of the photograph stands the village post office. Miss Sarah Ann Randle was sub-postmistress.

A pleasant view of the church of St Mary, Ashby Folville in 1905. The vicar and rural dean was Revd John Godson MA of St Catherine's College, Cambridge. He was also rural dean for the Goscate Division.

The Carington Arms public house in 1916, when John Alfred Walker was the publican.

Ashby Folville windmill in 1939. It was built between 1815 and 1826 and Hercules Brown was miller in 1891.

The remains of the tower in 1970, now used as an agricultural store.

Barsby post office in 1916. Albert Boden Platt, sub-postmaster and grocer, is standing in his shop doorway with family and friends. The building is now the Three Bows, a private house.

Bagrave End leading to Church Lane in 1906. Six Cottage Row is on the right of the photograph.

Barsby windmill in 1900, the remains of the post mill that ceased working in the late 1880s. Mr A. Greaves was miller in 1855.

Main Street, Gaddesby in 1916 with the Hermitage on the right.

Looking down Main Street toward the junction with Cross Street from outside of Hill Side in 1916.

The church of St Luke in 1910, when the vicar was the Revd Richard Quarry MA of Trinity College, Dublin.

Re-thatching what is now No. 17 Main Street in 1913. Opposite is the village blacksmith's forge.

The corner of Mill Lane and Great Lane, Frisby-on-the-Wreake in 1900. The thatched cottage to the right is now called Sunnyside Cottage.

A view of Main Street in 1900. The Black Horse public house is on the left. The landlord at that time was Austin Rodwell.

The market cross on Main Street in 1916. This view can be compared with the one below taken sixteen years earlier.

The market cross in 1900. To the left of the photograph is the workshop of Anthony and William Whitaker, saddlers.

The thatched cottage on Rotherby Lane in 1906. The cottage still stands showing very little alteration and is now called Zion House.

Main Street in 1904. A wheelbarrow stands outside the wheelwrights shop owned by Charles Edward Frisby. The sign for the Bell public house (licensee Robert Weston) is just visible in the centre background. On the right is the bakehouse run by Samuel Arthur Marriott.

Asfordby church and rectory in 1906. The vicar was the Revd John Charles Wellesley Burnaby MA of Trinity Hall, Cambridge.

Asfordby post office in 1936 when Thomas Charles Garland was postmaster. The adjacent tailors shop was run by Reginald Arthur Shilham.

The Primitive Methodist chapel in 1904. Built in 1840 and enlarged in 1884, it is now a butchers shop.

Asfordby Hall in 1928, the residence of Lady Theresa and Mr John Cross. In the 1960s the hall was converted to auction rooms and used by Mr Eric Startin. By 1970 the building had been demolished.

Main Street, Asfordby, April 1940, flooded by the waters of the Wreake.

Asfordby water-mill in 1932 just before it was demolished and the wheel sold for scrap. Tom Hives was the miller who ground corn in this water-mill in 1900.

Asfordby water-mill in 1904 when George Adkins was the miller. The mill house to the right of the photograph was the home of the Charles family in the 1930s.

A huntsman in full pursuit, riding across the fields near Holwell Ironworks in 1926. A detail from a painting by Charles Simpson RI.

Holwell Ironworks, *c.* 1920. The foundations for the first blast furnace were laid down in 1878. This came about as a result of the discovery in 1874 of large quantities of ironstone in the neighbouring villages of Holwell and Ab Kettleby by Mr Richard Dalgliesh. He formed the Holwell Iron Company in that year, naming it after the village of Holwell.

A dramatic photograph of the works taken in the 1950s. The first furnace was blown in 1881. Eventually ironstone was mined in the villages of Buckminster, South Witham, Sewstern and Market Overton to name but a few.

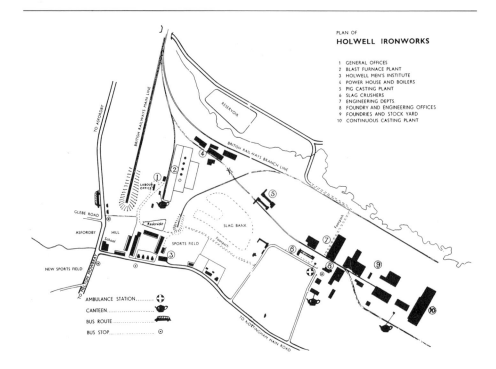

A plan of Holwell Ironworks.

Holwell Ironworks, 1950.

Shunting wagons containing scrap iron, prior to it being processed into pipes or metal inspection covers in 1969.

A view from the top of one of the furnaces in 1956 showing slag wagons in the background. A by-product of furnace production was crushed slag, graded and coated with tar, used as a road-surfacing aggregate. In 1950 3,000 tons per week were produced.

Holwell Works football team, 1951. Back row, left to right: Bert Perry, Walter Gunby, Jock Kerr, Dave Thomas, Derek Hack, Geoff Spiby. Front row: Raynor Garner, Vic Wright, Jimmy Learmonth, Bill Caithness, Norman Baxter.

Three Scotsmen playing for Holwell Works FC in the early 1950s. Left to right: Jimmy Learmonth, John Jardine, Bill Caithness.

The Army Dog Training Scheme kennels where the Royal Army Veterinary Corps dog training establishment was based.

'The Remount' at Welby, the army training camp for dogs and horses.

High Street, Ab Kettleby in 1910, looking towards the main Nottingham road.

Church Lane in 1904 with the spire of the church of St James just showing above the trees. The living was then held by the Revd Thomas Caleb Hughes of St Aidan's.

The elementary school, Ab Kettleby in 1910. Headmaster John Needham is standing to the right of a group of his pupils.

The headmaster of Ab Kettleby school, Mr John Needham, with his family in 1905.

The seven-arched pack-horse bridge at Rearsby in 1906, showing the ford in the fore-ground.

Old Hall, 1900, the seat of Henry Valentine Story Esq.

Station Lane in 1916. In the centre background stands Rearsby station with the signal box that controlled the level crossing just visible through the trees. Herbert J. Roberts was the station master.

Church Lane in 1916, leading to the church of St Michael. The vicar was the Revd Thomas Lionel George Hassall MA of Jesus College, Cambridge, and the sexton was Gordon Woodward.

Mill Road, *c.* 1925. The thatched cottage with a horse and cart standing in front of it is now No. 31.

Church Leys in 1916, the seat of Sir Hugo Meynell FitzHerbert Bt.

An Auster Aircraft Mk III manufactured by British Taylorcraft of Rearsby in 1943. This particular aircraft was on active duty with the British Eighth Army in Italy for artillery observation and liaison up to 19 July 1945.

Administrative buildings off Gaddesby Road, as used by Taylorcraft.

A meet of the Quorn hounds on the front lawn of Brooksby Hall in 1906. The hall was the home of Captain Gordon Chesney Wilson and Lady Sarah Spencer.

The head gardener's cottage at Brooksby Hall in 1906, the year the estate passed from the Wilson family to the Beattys, when it was purchased by Mrs Ethel Tree who married David Beatty.

Admiral of the Fleet Sir David Beatty in 1920 at the age of 49. He was the British Commander at the Battle of Jutland when the German fleet was routed on 31 May 1916.

Brooksby Hall in 1910, the residence of Rear Admiral Sir David Beatty CB, MYO, DSO.

The Hall gardens in 1910 with the church of St Michael in the background. Sir David Beatty on his retirement from the navy was created an earl and chose the title Baron Beatty of the North Sea and Brooksby.

The church of All Saints, Rotherby in 1904. The vicar was the Revd Edward Aden Beresford BA, LLM of King's College, Cambridge who resided at Hoby. Lady Sarah Wilson lived in the rectory next to the church.

Main Street, *c.* 1920. The gentleman holding the bicycle is standing in front of what is now No. 22.

The Hall in 1904, the home of Mrs Bell.

Rotherby Hall in 1925, now the home of John Cross Esq.

Hoby water-mill in 1874; a detail from a coloured print by John Sturgess. Lord Grey de Wilton, Mr G. Moore and the Revd Weller attempted to cross the plank bridge to the disused water-mill and splashed down into the River Wreake, so interrupting the hunt with the Quorn hounds being led by Tom Firr on Monday 16 February.

A general view of the village of Hoby from the Brooksby Road in 1904. In the centre background is the church of All Saints, where the vicar was the Revd Edward Aden Beresford MA, and the sexton John Mathers.

Cottages in front of the church of All Saints, *c.* 1900. The ivy-clad cottage in the centre of the picture is now No. 26, Sunny Bank, and the thatched cottage to the right has now been demolished and replaced with a house called Church View.

The elementary school, 1916, when Charles Wheatley was headmaster. The school was built in 1871.

Shoby Priory, farmed by Thomas Hallam in the 1940s.

Shoby House, farmed by George Hobill in the 1940s.

The Stocks, Grimston in 1910.

The elementary school in 1916. Mrs Annie Johnson was headmistress.

The church of St John with the Bishop and Sharpe tombstones positioned in one line.

The Black Horse public house and the post office in 1916. Arthur Wardle was the publican and William Botterill sub-postmaster.

The Park, 1904, the imposing residence of Charles William Wright Esq. JP.

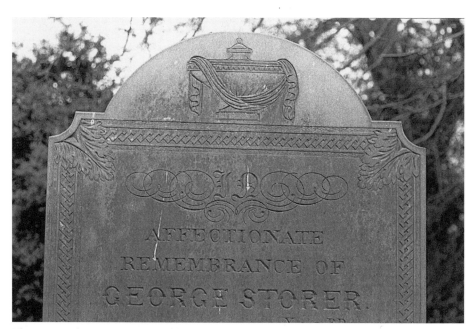

The grave of George Storer, a farmer and grazier in the parish of Saxelby during the middle of the nineteenth century, who died on 23 January 1864 aged 48 years.

The church of St Michael, annexed to Ab Kettleby, viewed through the branches of an ancient fallen walnut tree. The vicar in the 1940s was the Revd John Clulow Thompson.

The dovecot near the church.

Ragdale Hall, 1900, the home of the Hon. Alan Joseph Pennington and formerly the seat of the Earls Ferrers.

A general view of the village of Ragdale in 1904. The elementary school was maintained at the sole expense of Duke Storza-Cesarini. Miss Mary Skinner was headmistress and George Hamson was parish clerk.

School Lane, now Main Road, Old Dalby in 1916. The elementary school (now the village hall) is on the right. Thomas M. Hingley was headmaster. The cottage on the left is now called April Cottage.

Horses grazing on the village green in 1904, seven years after the sapling standing in front of the ivy-clad cottage (background, right) was planted to commemorate the Diamond Jubilee of Queen Victoria. This tree, a Spanish oak, has flourished and now has a trunk 4 ft across and dominates this area of the village.

Church Lane in 1916, with the church of St Martin in the middle distance. The sexton was Robert Peel.

St Martin's church in 1925, when the living was held by the Revd Reginald Sydney Carruthers Hawthorn Wood MA of St John's College, Cambridge. To the left of the photograph is the private entrance to Old Dalby Hall which, in 1925, was the seat of Charles James Phillips Esq. DL, JP. He was a principal shareholder in Watneys Brewery and was regularly conveyed through these gates in a 'coach and four'.

Chapel Lane, Nether Broughton in 1900, named after the Wesleyan chapel built in 1839.

Nether Broughton post office in 1904, looking from King Street. Charles George Milnes was sub-postmaster. This thatched post office has long since been demolished but the present post office is situated next door in the row of terraced houses.

The church of St Mary with the memorial to the village lads who gave their lives in the First World War.

The Anchor Inn on the main Nottingham road in 1956. Tom Crook was the licensee in 1936.

Section Three
THE BURROUGH
ESCARPMENT AND
SETTLEMENTS TO THE SOUTH

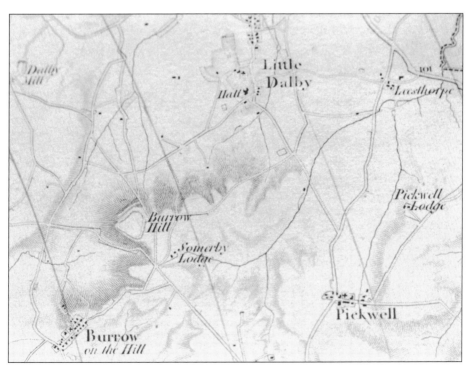

Section of the 1835 edition of the Ordnance Survey, revised in 1867.

The Green, Top End in 1910, with the church of St Swithin in the background. The Revd Robert Carthew Dashwood MA was vicar, the sexton was Joel Sharpe.

Coats of arms high up on the south side of St Swithin's. On the left, quartered three lions of England, passant and the fleur-de-lis of France, ancient and modern. Right, Thomas de Brotherton, Earl of Norfolk.

Eye Kettleby water-mill, *c.* 1850. The mill ceased operating during the First World War and was purchased and demolished by the district council in the 1920s so that they could control the water rights.

A detail from a painting by Rigby Graham, 1969, of the remains of the bomb aiming tower which was part of the training area on Dalby Aerodrome.

LAC Jack Williamson, stationed at Dalby Aerodrome. In 1944 he was awarded a life-saving certificate for assisting in the rescue of the crew of a plane which crashed off Saxby Road, Melton Mowbray at Copley's South, now an industrial estate.

A view of the control tower at Dalby Aerodrome in 1967. This tower, built as an experimental unit, was unique in the whole of Britain. It should never have been demolished in the 1970s.

The successful RAF football team that represented Melton Mowbray (Dalby Aerodrome) in the 1943/4 season. Back row, left to right: MacDonald, Casson, Reg David, -?-, -?-, Fred Butcher. Front row: Bill Gould, Jimmy Learmonth, Bert Broadhurst, Fred Moon, Jack Smith.

Three RAF personnel in 1944 near the hanger that stood adjacent to Great Dalby village. Left to right: Jimmy Learmonth, Ian Hunter and their friend Alan.

The grandstand for the 1900 Burton races. As is apparent from the photograph, this was a highly fashionable venue, nobility patronizing the event.

The ring at Burton races in 1912. Lord Glentanor resided at the manor house nearby.

Thorpe Satchville Hall in 1905, owned by John Otho Paget and occupied by Henry Harrison Parry and F.H.K. Durlacher.

The Pinfold, 1905, owned by Frederick Kneeling Durlacher.

Little Dalby Hall, 1904, the residence of Mrs Burns-Hartopp, lady of the manor, and her husband Capt. James Burns-Hartopp JP, MFH.

Little Dalby Hall, 1903. This hall, built in the Elizabethan period, was extensively restored in 1838 and 1851. This photograph was used as a postcard, and on the reverse is the comment that the sender is about to commence making the Stilton cheese for Christmas.

White House Farm on the junction of Loseby Lane and Burrough Road, Twyford, 1905.

Main Road in 1910, with Brook House on the left and the cheese dairy in the middle distance, which was demolished during the Second World War by a runaway army lorry.

Town Bridge on Main Road, *c*. 1905. On the skyline top left stands Twyford Windmill, a post mill.

Main Street in 1910 with the Odd Fellows Hall, built in 1908, on the right. It is now the village hall.

The edge of the escarpment of Burrough Hill, 690 ft above sea level. The hill is the site of an Iron Age encampment.

Main Street, Burrough on the Hill, leading to Somerby, in 1910.

The church of St Mary with the rectory in the foreground, 1916. The rector was the Revd John M. Gedan MA.

The junction with Main Street and Newbold gated road in 1910. The entrance to Burrough House is in the background, to the left.

Ashleigh House on Main Street, Somerby in 1905.

Somerby House in 1905, occupied by Charles Edward Hay Esq.

The Grove in 1905, when it was occupied by Major Augustus Candy.

High Street, *c.* 1950. A girl on a pony is standing outside the village school with the local garage in the centre background.

Stooks of corn standing in 'Red-earth' Pickwell in the 1920s.

Pickwell war memorial, *c.* 1950.

All Saints' church, Pickwell, viewed from the rectory garden in 1910.

The rectory at Pickwell in 1908. The Revd Charles James Petne Blundell MA was the incumbent.

The north side of Leesthorpe Hall in 1908, the seat of Francis Sloane Stanley Esq. DL, JP.

Cottesmore hounds at a meet in the park on the south side of Leesthorpe Hall in 1928. The Hall was then the seat of John W. Burns Esq. JP. The Master of Fox Hounds was James Baird Esq.

The junction to Knossington and Somerby, Cold Overton in 1905.

Cold Overton Hall in 1916, the seat of James F. Montagu Esq.

Frederick Holmes' farm cart standing on the Somerby Road in 1925.

The gated road to Whissendine in 1905.

The Greyhound public house, Knossington in 1906. Mrs Martha Weatherstone was the licensee.

The elementary school in 1906, erected in 1899 by A.L. Duncan Esq. for £1,500. In 1906 Archie Looker was headmaster, and Miss Susan Weatherstone the infants mistress.

'Whalebones' on Main Street in 1916.

The entrance to 'Whalebones' opposite the Braunston Road on Main Street in 1905. On the left is the home of farmer and grazier Evan Louis Evans Esq.

Knossington Mill in 1895 when William Gale was the miller. This tower mill was erected in 1849 by Mr E. Clarke.

The remains of Knossington Mill in 1970 when the base was being used as a farm store. No trace of this mill now exists.

Section Four
ALONG THE RIVER EYE

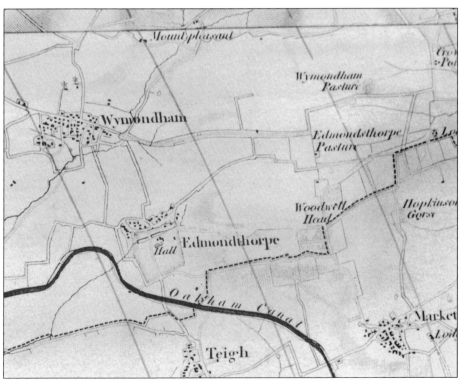

Section of the 1835 edition of the Ordnance Survey, revised in 1867.

The headstone over the grave of Robert Thorpe Chamberlain, in the graveyard of St Mary the Virgin at Wyfordby. He was parish clerk for thirty-three years and sub-postmaster up until his death in 1893 aged 80.

Gangers' 'bothy' at Brentingby in the spring of 1965.

Greengate ford bridge over the River Eye, 1966. This was constructed by the Oakham Canal Company in the 1790s to carry horse-drawn vehicles over the river to the adjacent bridge that spanned the Melton to Oakham canal. For very many years it was maintained by the Midland Railway Company.

Brentingby crossing gatehouse on the edge of the Peterborough to Nottingham railway in 1933. The crossing keeper was responsible for opening the crossing gates on the field road leading to Greengate ford bridge and the polo ground beyond. In the 1920s and '30s this was a 'mecca' for the royalty and nobility who spent the season in the Melton Mowbray district supporting the three local hunts.

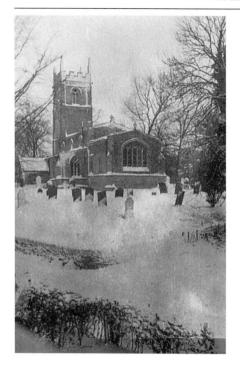

The church of St Mary in the winter of 1947. Freeby village was cut off from the outside world for nearly six weeks because of drifting snow.

Graham and Pamela Mason sitting on a farm dray at the boundary fence to 'Beckam's' in the autumn of 1947.

An aerial view of farm buildings and Brook Cottages at the east end of Freeby village in the late 1960s.

Pamela Mason with her 'cade' lamb, a familiar sight on Freeby main street during the summer of 1949.

The thatched cottage on the Garthorpe road, Saxby in the 1920s. Charlie Skerritt is on the right and his daughter Fanny is on the far left of the group. This picturesque building was demolished by Buckminster Estates many years ago.

His Majesty King Edward VII standing on Saxby station on the Nottingham–Peterborough line, in 1907, waiting for his Sandringham connection.

Alice Smith of Saxby in 1927. Note the neck-
lace of hand-marbled wooden beads.

Abram Smith servicing his steam traction engine in 1925.

Mile post on the towpath of the Melton to Oakham canal in 1965. This canal was opened in 1803 and closed in 1847 when it was purchased by the Midland Railway Company.

Alice Smith and Bill Mason haymaking in the summer of 1926.

Roasting an ox at Garthorpe in the paddock at the junction of the Coston to Saxby road in 1897 to celebrate the Diamond Jubilee of Queen Victoria.

Castle mound and ditch on the edge of the River Eye at Garthorpe in 1969. These defensive earthworks, with water-filled ditch and palisade of sharpened stakes, were 'thrown up' throughout the country as a matter of expedience during the anarchic reign of Stephen (1135–54) and relied chiefly on their height and the strength of the earthern ramparts.

Coston water-mill in the 1890s. Remains of this mill can still be seen next to the ford on the Sproxton road.

The blue brick bridge over the River Eye. The brick cottage in the background was built by the Earl of Dysart in 1884.

Main Street, Buckminster, 1904. Thompson Skins stands outside his blacksmiths shop with his assistant and several onlookers. In the background on the left stands the Dysart Arms Hotel. Arthur Wells was the proprietor.

William (Trump) Farley at the controls of his locomotive pulling loaded wagons off the edge of the opencast ironstone working near Buckminster cricket ground in the 1950s.

Buckminster Hall in 1916, erected in 1798 and the seat of the Earl of Dysart. It was demolished in the 1950s and a new hall has been built on the site.

The entrance to the stables in 1904, part of the estate owned by the Earl of Dysart. William Weston was harness maker to the earl.

Loading ironstone with a drag line into wagons near the Colsterworth road in 1956.

Sharon Hickman of Wymondham on George Slack's pony at Buckminster Gymkhana in 1964.

The Bede Houses near the River Eye at Stapleford in 1939. The buildings were extensively restored in 1992.

Jack Pickaver, blacksmith, repairing a pump in the forge at Stapleford in 1965. Harry Taylor is on the bellows, keeping up the heat so necessary for good ironwork production.

The two principal actors from *The Avengers* of ABC Television making a film in Stapleford Park in 1965. The Hall is in the background, the lake is on the left, and John Steed (Patrick MacNee) is untying Emma Peel (Diana Rigg) in the nick of time to save her from a gruesome death at the hands of villains of the foulest kind.

A working model of the SS *Northern Star* cruising on the lake in Stapleford Park in the summer of 1963.

The main entrance to Stapleford Hall in 1925, the seat of Lieut.-Col. John Gretton CBE, VD, MP, JP, lord of the manor.

Peter Pepper with his Priestman Dragline excavator, prior to his partially cleaning out the lake in 1958 using an 8 cu. ft bucket.

The Three Horse Shoes public house on the main street, Wymondham in 1904, when the publican was Daniel Burton.

The Rookery in 1916, the residence of John P. Grenfell Esq.

Edmondthorpe and Wymondham railway station in 1904 when John Cook was the station master. The spire of the church of St Peter can be seen in the background. The vicar at the time was the Revd William Hill Lee MA of Christ's College, Cambridge.

A Midland and Great Northern Johnson 4–4–0 in Wymondham railway station in 1937 waiting for passengers to board.

Wymondham windmill in 1904. Thomas Oldham was the miller.

The millstone floor in 1970, seen during
the extensive restoration programme.

Sycamore House in 1904, then the residence of Richard Louis Fenwick who was married to the actress Sylvia Gray. Just visible to the left is the oak tree planted in 1887 to commemorate Queen Victoria's Golden Jubilee.

Wymondham Odd Fellows Club parade outside the Hunters Arms, *c.* 1910. Mr George Duffin is standing at the horse's head. The passengers on the Ellis and Everard's delivery dray are, left to right: Gwen Bellamy, Maria Townsend, Sybil Saunders, Esther Naylor, Harriet Tysoe and Edith Pickaver. The publican of the Hunters Arms was Edward Charles Saunders.

Wymondham Dairy, 1910, manufacturers of fine Stilton cheese. Left to right: Mrs Bratby, Miss Briggs, Mrs W. Harris, Miss S. Chafer (manageress).

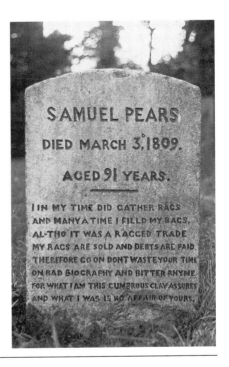

The headstone of Samuel Pears in Wymondham churchyard, positioned a few yards west of the church tower. Known as 'the Rag Man's Grave', this headstone was erected at the expense of Revd Richard Cragg who also wrote the poem engraved upon the stone. Samuel Pears was married four times and was a legend in his own lifetime.

Inside the control gondola of the *Schütte-Lanz* airship of the German Imperial Army that bombed Paines railway sidings, in the parish of Wymondham, on 3 September 1916.

The goods yard at Wymondham railway station in 1918. The people at the depot of Herbert Whait, coal merchant of Melton Mowbray are, left to right: Robert Barfoot (Whait's agent in Wymondham), Henry Naylor (horseman, sitting), Tom Fisher (horseman, standing).

The Blue Dog public house on the main street, Sewstern in 1916. The publican was Thomas Arthur Wilson.

School Lane in 1916. On the left of the photograph stands Brook Cottages, built in 1913, and behind this building stands Grange House, built in 1893. The row of cottages on the right has been demolished.

The Wesleyan chapel in 1916. The chapel was built in 1904 at a cost of £600.

'Jason' in the loco sheds situated off Gunby Road in 1966.

The hollow elm tree standing in front of Edmondthorpe post office in 1904 when Miss Emma Worsdale was sub-postmistress. In the background on the right stands the elementary school erected in 1838 and extensively rebuilt at the expense of William Ann Pochin Esq. in 1863. The headmistress was Miss Edith Ellen Booth.

The only surviving bridge on the Melton to Oakham canal, 1965. This bridge originally carried vehicles on the road from Teigh to Edmondthorpe; now it is just an access point to two fields.

School House in 1907, then the home of Miss Edith Ellen Booth, headmistress of the elementary school.

The gardens of School House, 1907. Miss Edith Ellen Booth sits in the front of the group and her brother, Syd Booth, stands at the back.

Clearing snow on the Wymondham to Edmondthorpe road in 1947. From left to right: Mr Jack Welbourn, Mr E. Veasey, Mr Gerry Potter, Mr A. Pepper. The roads in this parish were completely blocked by drifting snow for seven weeks.

The decorated font in the church of St Michael and All Angels in 1965. The vicar was the Revd John Lawrence Vincent Houghton.

The Smith monument in Edmondthorpe church. The lower alabaster figure is Lady Ann Smith; the effigy has a red stain on the left wrist and under certain circumstances is said to 'bleed'. She was considered to be a witch and capable of turning herself into a white cat. The white cat was caught thieving in the kitchen by the cook and its left paw was slashed with a cleaver. From that day onwards the lady of the house carried a red scar on her left wrist.

Edmondthorpe Hall in 1791, the seat of William Pochin Esq., from an engraving by John Throsby.

Edmondthorpe Hall in 1904, the residence of Victoria Alexandrina, Dowager Countess of Yarborough and John Maunsell-Richardson Esq.

The remains of Edmondthorpe Hall in 1965. The magnificent Hall was burnt down in 1943 while occupied by British soldiers; the result of an incident in the kitchen with the army cook, a white cat, a candle and a pan of fat!

Whissendine station, Edmondthorpe. A photograph of a colour print by John Sturgess involving the Cottesmore Hunt on 20 March 1879. Ignoring the pleas of the crossing keeper, Captain Stirling, Mr George Finch and others decided to take a short cut to Wymondham Roughs along the railway, with disastrous results.

Whissendine station on the Peterborough to Nottingham railway line in 1965. The half-timbered ticket office has now been demolished.

Section Five
TOWARDS THE
VALE OF BELVOIR AND
HIGH LEICESTERSHIRE

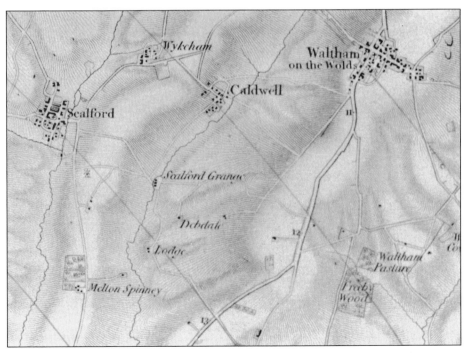

Section of the 1835 edition of the Ordnance Survey, revised in 1867.

The junction of Hose Lane with Waltham Lane, Long Clawson in 1904. Elms Farm lies directly behind the signpost, with Sunnycroft to the right of the photograph.

The centre of the east end of the village in 1904. The Sands is to the right of the photograph. Pack House on the left had only just been built. The house in the centre is Lynwood and the shop across the road on the right is now Lumb and Co., Butchers.

Long Clawson windmill in 1935, a six-storeyed brick tower mill built in the early 1800s on the site of an earlier mill. John Henry Shilcock was the miller in 1916. It ceased working as a windmill during the First World War.

A parking area off The Sands, *c.* 1902. The house on the left has now been demolished and the village surgery is built on the site. The post office, which was run by John Bissell Millar, can be seen behind the parish notice-board. Mr Millar also ran the bakery next door.

The Crown and Plough in 1904, when Albine Knapp was the publican. He was also the carrier to Nottingham on Saturday and Melton Mowbray on Tuesday. The cottage on the right has been demolished and the village hall now stands on the site.

Long Clawson Dairy Ltd in 1932. The dairy, managed by William McNair, manufactured prime Stilton cheese.

The Wesleyan chapel in 1932. The chapel was built in 1840 and stands next door to the manse, where John Wesley Thornley lived.

The church of St Remigius in 1932. The vicar was the Revd George Douglas Jordan BA of Leeds University. This photograph also shows the Primitive Methodist chapel built in 1868.

West End Stores in 1932.

The church of St Michael, Hose in 1904, when the Revd John Williams of St Bees was the vicar. In the centre of the photograph stands the elementary school built in 1845. Henry Martin was headmaster.

The Baptist chapel in 1928. It was built in 1818 and was licensed for marriages.

The church of St Michael viewed from the village green in 1936. The living was held by the Revd Frederick Appleton of University College, Durham.

The bridge over the Grantham Canal at Hose in 1928. William Jessop presented a bill to Parliament in 1792 to construct a canal from Nottingham to Grantham. After many difficulties had been overcome, the whole length of the canal was opened for navigation in 1797.

The Methodist chapel, Harby in 1904, built in 1847.

The elementary school was erected in 1860 and could accommodate 120 boys and girls. It is pictured here in 1904 when Alfred Warman Edwards was headmaster.

Harby village, *c.* 1938, with the war memorial to the lads of the village who gave their lives in the First World War and the village school built in 1860.

Dickman's Lane in the 1960s. The converted cottages on this lane are now named Trevelyans Cottage.

Harby windmill in 1900. Messrs Lamin and Shipman were the millers, grinding corn and manufacturing cattle-cake for local use.

An interior view of the stone floor inside Harby mill in 1939 showing a pair of stones. In 1937 the mill was purchased by Dickman and Wolley who ground pig and cattle feed for their own use and for sale to local farmers. In 1938 the mill was 'tail-winded'; it was not repaired and the owners sold the machinery for scrap. When Langer Aerodrome was built the mill was in the direct flight path and the top two floors were therefore removed.

The Red Lion on Red Lion Street, Stathern, viewed from the Toft in 1904. Thomas Hart was the publican.

Thatched cottages off The Green in 1904. All these buildings have now been demolished except for Peck's Homestead, the last cottage in the row on the left.

A signal box on the railway sidings serving the local opencast mines in 1966.

Looking towards Bottesford from Stathern ironstone railway sidings in 1966.

The church of St Guthlac in 1904, when the vicar was the Revd John William Taylor MA, JP of St Peter's College, Cambridge. Laburnam House is the white house in the centre, with Mill House to the left.

The remains of the base of Stathern post mill in 1955. The wooden body of the mill had been removed before 1900, and the roundhouse has now been completely demolished. The last recorded millers were William Rowten and Robert Starbuck in 1892.

The entrance to the ironstone mine at Holwell in 1885.

The ancient chapelry with one bell. The vicar of Ab Kettleby would officiate at services here.

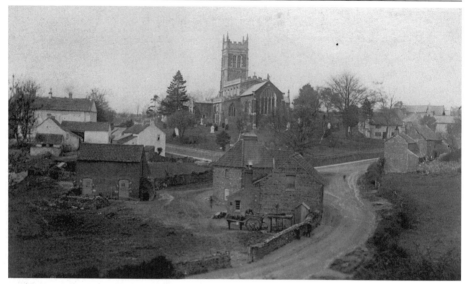

A general view of Scalford in 1900. The church of St Egelwin the Martyr is in the centre background. The vicar was the Revd Henry Twells Mogridge MA of St Peter's College, Cambridge, and the sexton was Benjamin Pearson. William Wilford Whittle was clerk to the parish council. Scalford Dairy, producer of fine Stilton cheese, is in the foreground.

The Primitive Methodist chapel built in 1870 and viewed from King Street in 1904. Further down the street is the Kings Arms, where James Watchorn was the publican and, in the middle distance, The Plough, where the publican was Richard Graves Pollard.

The headstone of John Morris's grave in Scalford churchyard. He lived at the Manor House, Wymondham, and was buried in the family plot at Scalford. The Morris family were farmers and cheese manufacturers, John's nephew successfully running the Wymondham Dairy, producer of fine Stilton cheese.

Scalford station in the 1930s, a class J39 train passing through on the way to Leicester. Stilton cheese was conveyed direct to the House of Commons in London via this station prior to the Second World War.

Church Street in 1900. The imposing building to the left of centre is the post office, William Wright the sub-postmaster.

The Wesleyan chapel in 1904. This large chapel was built in 1844.

The undenominational mission room erected in 1896 at Wycomb.

The chapel of St Mary built before 1300 in the Norman style in the fields at Chadwell.

Goadby Hall in 1900, the seat of Lady Henrietta Turner and Algernon Turner Esq. CB, JP. Their farm bailiff was William Moseley.

The school, erected in 1861 at a cost of £350, was paid for by a former rector of the church of St Denys.

The approach to Eastwell village in the 1950s.

A sign indicating Eastwell Quarries in 1966.

The engine sheds at Eastwell Quarries on top of Harby Hill in 1966. The rails ran down to Stathern ironstone railway sidings.

A cable-operated incline at Eastwell in 1959 conveying iron ore from the quarries to the British Rail main railhead and sidings.

A general view of Eaton in 1916, with the embattled Norman tower of St Denis sitting high on the skyline. The vicar was the Revd James Henry Moore MA of Durham University, and the parish clerk was Thomas Pearson.

Eaton Grange in 1916, the seat of Major George C.B. Paynter DSO.

'Rutland' standing in the mineral railway sidings at Eaton before the First World War.

A British Rail branch line, showing the timber viaduct near Eaton in 1955.

'Nantes' in full steam near Eaton in 1955. Built in France, this engine came to the Waltham Quarries in 1934.

Two locals standing outside The Wheel Inn, Branston in 1904 when Miss Ann Hand was the publican. In the centre background two people can just be discerned. They are Harry Clifford and Mrs George.

Branston church in 1928. The living from the church of St Guthlac is annexed to Croxton Kerrial whose vicar was the Revd John Henry Evans BA of St David's College, Lampeter. Stephen Malcolm Pilkington was living in the rectory, which is now covered in ivy and looks very different from the photograph on the next page. An alcove in the church wall holds the recently installed war memorial.

The elementary school, erected in 1843. Miss Orpah Murrell was headmistress when this photograph was taken in 1916.

Branston Rectory in 1906. The vicar for the parish was the Revd David Vilkie Peregrine BA, LTh of University College, Durham, appointed in 1905. He was also rural dean for the Framland division.

The crossroads in the centre of Waltham-on-the-Wolds in 1904. The Royal Horse Shoes public house, whose licensee was William Edwin Rose, is on the right.

Melton Road in 1916. The spire of the church of St Mary Magdalene is just visible above the trees. The vicar was the Revd Bertell Hubert Smith MA of Durham University, and the parish clerk and sexton was William Clark. On the left are the stone pillars indicating the entrance to the elementary school, erected in 1844; George Higgens was headmaster at the time of the photograph.

The windmill in 1925, when the miller was Edward Robinson. This mill was built on the site of a post mill in 1868. The Robinson family had been millers and ground corn in mills on this site continuously for over 100 years. It was sold to Richard and Walter Owen in the 1920s.

The spur wheel driving the stone-nut, 1938.   The feed leading to the millstone, 1938.

High Street, 1916. The house on the right is Stoneleigh and the sign of The Wheel public house is just visible at the end of the roadway. The licensee in 1916 was Mrs Sarah Ann Lock.

Waltham-on-the-Wolds signal box on the Great Northern branch line from Scalford in the 1940s. This was mainly a goods line, but when the Croxton Park racecourse was in full use a passenger service was introduced solely for the event.

An ancient drinking trough for cattle and horses at the entrance to Race Course Farm, Bescaby.

The gable end of a typical cottage built in the nineteenth century for farm workers and their families.

A general view of Croxton Kerrial in 1904, with the church of St John the Baptist in the middle distance. The vicar at the time was the Revd William Ernest Pelham Malden BA of Trinity College, Cambridge. The parish clerk was William Charity.

Main Street in 1916. Charles John Prowse was headmaster at the elementary school, built in 1844. Miss Laura Prowse and Miss Letitia Adams were assistants. The Peacock Inn stands at the end of the street. Robert Knott was the publican.

Croxton Kerrial smock mill in 1905. In the foreground is the last miller, Newman Shire, busy feeding his hens and turkeys.

Croxton Kerrial village in 1905, with the parish pump in the centre foreground. The smock mill in the background would appear to be unique as it was the only one built in this style in Leicestershire. It had a boat-shaped cap.

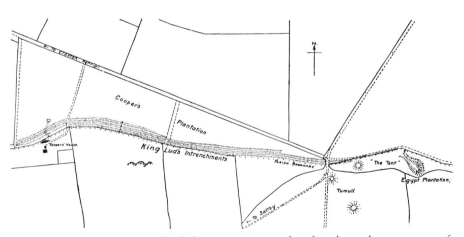

King Lud's entrenchments. This defence system stretches for about three-quarters of a mile along the parish boundary with Saltby. It is a ditch and rampart fortification to defend a kingdom against advancing armies. Legend ascribes it to the Bronze Age, some 3,000 years ago, when King Lud was involved in what can only be described as 'trench warfare'.

The centre of Stonesby in 1904. The church of St Peter stands high in the background. The vicar of Waltham-on-the-Wolds held the living, and the parish clerk was Thomas Bursnall. Henry Hickman ran the grocers and drapers shop near the church.

A typical red pantiled roof so common in this area of Leicestershire. The tower behind is that of St Peter's church.

The Nags Head public house standing at the crossroads in the centre of Saltby in 1904. Alfred Henry Skinner was the publican; he also ran the local shop.

High Street in 1916. The Nags Head public house is on the right, where Townsend Pretty was the publican.

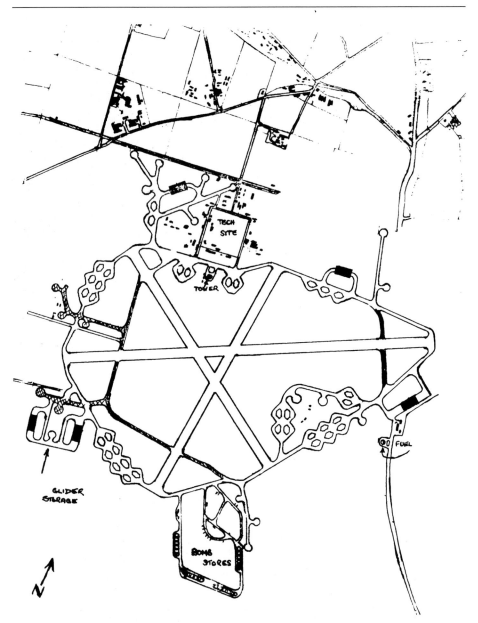

A plan of Saltby Aerodrome, a satellite of Cottesmore. Built in the early 1940s, it was a base for the American Air Force who flew Flying Fortresses out of it on many successful raids on occupied Europe. It was also one of the many aerodromes that were staging bases for the glider invasion of northern France in support of the D-Day landings.

A detail from a line and wash illustration by Rigby Graham, 1969, showing the remains of the bomb aiming tower which was part of the training area on Saltby aerodrome.

The main control tower on Saltby Aerodrome, 1969.

The squadron insignia made by American airmen in the 1940s on the approach road to Saltby Aerodrome in 1970. The roadside verge where it lay has since been altered.

Gliders on Saltby Aerodrome, now part of the aerial scene in this part of Leicestershire.

The elementary school, Sproxton in 1916, when the headmaster was Francis Joseph Warham. The school was built in 1871 for 100 children. It has since been converted into the village hall.

The post office in 1916 when Ernest Harry Trayford was sub-postmaster and grocer. The Crown public house is visible to the left of centre in the background. Henry Joel Tarratt was the publican.

British Rail line to Sproxton Quarries, looking down the line from Crabtree Lane bridge in 1966.

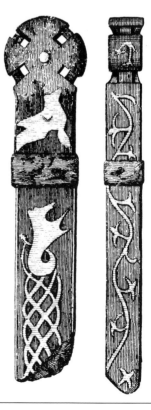

Carvings on the Saxon cross that stands in the graveyard at the church of St Bartholomew, Sproxton.

Sproxton post mill in the early 1920s. J. Pridmore was the miller in 1916. It stopped work in 1920 and was demolished in 1949 to make way for the Sproxton opencast iron ore workings.

The brake wheel, windshaft and stone-nut inside Sproxton post mill in 1939.

Acknowledgements

To compile a book of this type would not be possible without the help of many kind and well disposed individuals. The basis of this collection of old photographs has been the author's own extensive collection, and it is presumed that all the photographs from this source are out of copyright. Should this not be the case, Trevor Hickman offers his sincere apologies for reproducing them without permission and will make an acknowledgement in future publications. Collections such as his are made over very many years and, first and foremost, the author thanks his wife Pamela for her continued patience for over thirty years spent with a passionate collector of local history ephemera and publications. Inspiration came from many sources and the author's good friend, the artist Rigby Graham, has provided considerable help over the years. He allowed the author to use photographs taken by him and to reproduce two photographs of his paintings, one of which is in the collection of Mike Goldmark. Nigel Moon, the enthusiastic miller, would have filled the book with photographs of mills, mill machinery and mineral railway lines with locomotives in full steam. Many of the photographs showing these subjects have been provided by Nigel. Photographs of Holwell Works and information are from the author's late father-in-law, Bill Mason, with whom he spent many enjoyable hours discussing local industry and farming in this area of Leicestershire. Thanks are due to Mr and Mrs A. Charles for their professional help over many years and also for allowing the author to reproduce photographs of Asfordby, Kirby Bellars and Melton Mowbray extracted from their private collection. David Burton of Stroud provided information on Melton families; unfortunately, due to lack of space, only one photograph has been reproduced. Chris Salter of Midland Counties Publications found the photograph of the Auster aircraft reproduced on p. 49. Lady Gretton has very kindly allowed the reproduction of photographs taken by her late husband, John, of interesting features associated with Stapleford Park. Jimmy Learmonth provided considerable information on Dalby Aerodrome and uncovered many photographs of football teams associated with this aerodrome and with Holwell Works. The Squire de Lisle found the photograph of the Prince of Wales, reproduced on p. 19, in his extensive collection. Thanks are also due to all those people in so many villages that the author visited in the spring of 1992 who willingly offered advice and help in identifying the sites depicted in many of the photographs. Finally, thanks to Jenny Weston, who converted the author's awful handwritten text into a neat typescript for the publisher.

Part Two
MELTON MOWBRAY

In Full Flight by Charles Simpson

An engraving of a drawing by John Throsby, originally published on 30 January 1790. This is possibly the earliest printed and published view of Melton Mowbray. Two farmers are shown approaching the town along what is now Scalford Road. One is riding a packhorse with panniers laden with Stilton cheese for sale at the weekly market in the town centre, held near the church of St Mary.

Contents

A Bad Fall, by John Sturgess.

The Golden Age of the Pictorial Postcard

Edwardian Melton Mowbray: the cobbled main street, Sherrard Street, *c.* 1907. The photographer stood on Thorpe End, opposite Thomas Moore's bakehouse, with the Marquis of Granby public house to the left and the infamous *pissoir* opposite. This was removed because of public outcry: it caused offence to the ladies of the town on most days, especially when the street market was held adjacent to the structure on Tuesdays. It was not helped by the gas lamp overhanging the cast-iron enclosure, illuminating the users through the decorated iron grilles in the early evening, and of course late into the night, when revellers from the public house opposite made use of the facility.

Introduction

This is a companion to *Around Melton Mowbray in Old Photographs*. It is not a history of the town but a selection of the old and not so old photographs that have been collected over a number of years by me and many of my friends, some of whom have helped with the book's preparation. Their names are recorded in the acknowledgements.

Melton Mowbray is a typical small Midlands market town, seemingly no different to other similar towns. It is only once you delve into the history of the area that you realize it is unique. Being a photographic collection, this history should commence in the late nineteenth century, but to add interest I have included photographs of prints, paintings and monuments that date back many centuries. The frontispiece is a detail of an eighteenth-century engraving showing two farmers approaching the town on the way to the local market just as farmers have done since before the Domesday Survey (1084–6), when the market that had been controlled by Geoffrey de Wirce since 1077 showed a return of twenty shillings per annum. Our market certainly dates from the Saxon period and has probably been held on a Tuesday for over a thousand years. The engraving shows St Mary's church standing high in the background as it has done since the thirteenth century. The artist illustrates a collection of thatched houses in the centre of the town, and on the extreme left stands a well built stone structure which could be The Limes built by Robert Hudson early in the 1600s and, like so many fine buildings in this town, demolished in this century in the name of progress.

Unfortunately that is the story of this market town: build, expand, destroy and build again. Could it have been any different? I doubt it. The town is a centre for trade and as such must cater to the demands of the merchants, the retailers and their customers. Fashions and the demand for locally produced goods change, so the town must change. The market has expanded over the centuries and, thankfully, it still does today. The fine fifteenth- and sixteenth-century houses built by merchants were all to be demolished. One of our finest local architects and builders, Christopher Staveley, *demolished* in 1780 the Mansion House that stood on the site of the present day St Mary's Way car park. Before the Mansion House was built the fortified Manor House of the Mowbrays, where King Richard Coeur de Lion stayed in 1194, stood in this area.

I have experienced considerable sadness looking at so many photographs of buildings that have been demolished in my lifetime, in some instances quite wantonly to my mind, but not of course to that of the town planners who must ensure that the prosperity of a thousand years continues. Growth is so important. This is a thriving market town, not a 'fossilized tourist centre relying on an interest in the past to generate income'. Historic buildings *can* blend in with modern interests, but not, I regret to say, in Melton Mowbray. It seems wrong and short sighted to me to have demolished the three Round Houses on Sage Cross Street, Woodville, the canal surveyor's house, and Thomas Moore's bakehouse on Thorpe End, and Elgin Lodge, that was John Ferneley's Studio. All these have gone since 1950 to be replaced with no substantial structure of modern architecture that could blend into the town of the future. What a tourist attraction these buildings would be now!

This then is a photographic record of much that has gone. I have included people wherever possible and have devoted one section to personalities in the town. For further reading on the history of this unique market town I suggest a browse through the pages of the following three books: *Melton Mowbray in Olden Times* by J. Ward (1879), *The Story of Melton Mowbray* by P.E. Hunt (1957), *Melton Mowbray, Queen of the Shires* by J. Brownlow (1980).

Having spent three years at school in the town, and worked at J.W. Warners at 2 South Parade for eleven years, all in the late 1940s and throughout the 1950s, I have witnessed many changes. At the time, as I have said, they were considered essential to the continuing prosperity of the town. My interest in the history of Melton Mowbray was generated by three people: John Greenslade, who appears on some of the 'official' photographs in this book; Norman Brooks, my works manager at Warners, who is standing in the centre of the group in the photograph on p. 126 (without Norman's interest none of the 1950s photographs of Chappie and Petfoods would have survived), and Jack Brownlow. In 1979 I helped Jack publish his marvellous book on Melton Mowbray; his knowledge of the history of the town was incredible.

From what we would now call a small village the town has grown into the urban community we inhabit today. A centre for the sale of agricultural products in the Saxon period, it became involved in the wool trade during the medieval period. With the sixteenth- and seventeenth-century enclosures the agriculture-based economy of the area changed and cheese made its appearance. The arrival of the canals in the late eighteenth century opened up the area at the same time as fox hunting as a spectacular rural sport arrived. The hunters of foxes were instrumental in widening the market for stilton cheese and pork pies and the manufacture of these products expanded during the nineteenth century and continues to do so today. The prosperity of the town was maintained by the mining and processing of iron ore in the early part of this century. The manufacture of pet foods by an internationally famous food processing company since the early 1950s has ensured the prosperity of the town continues.

Seal of John de Mowbray on a conveyance for a parcel of land purchased by Robert, son of Richard of Waltham, in December 1341. This land was located along the banks of the River Eye, near Brentingby.

Produce of the Town and District

The famous Melton Mowbray pork pie, developed in and around Melton Mowbray in farmhouse kitchens, butchers' and bakers' shops and peasants' cottages, through the sixteenth, seventeenth, eighteenth and into the nineteenth centuries. Discovered by the wealthy foxhunters who patronised the town from the late eighteenth century onwards, the pies were promoted by Edward Adcock from his bakehouse in Back Lane next to the Fox Inn in 1831. They were marketed in London as Melton Mowbray pork pies.

Stilton cheese was named after the small town that is situated approximately 70 miles north of London on the Great North Road. Developed in the village of Wymondham in the late sixteenth century, it was marketed in Stilton; shortly after 1700 the cheese was promoted by Cooper Thornhill who kept the Bell Inn at Stilton. Frances Pawlett, a Wymondham cheese maker, was his main supplier. For further reading please see *The History of Stilton Cheese*, Sutton Publishing, 1996.

Section One
The Town

Melton Mowbray! Detail from the first published road atlas by Emanuel Bowen in 1720.

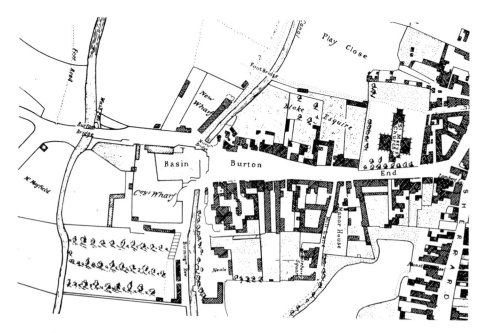

Plan of Burton Street (Burton End), *c.* 1840. This part of the town experienced considerable change with the building of the railway in the 1840s.

The canal bridge viewed from the New Wharf, looking into the Basin, *c.* 1870.

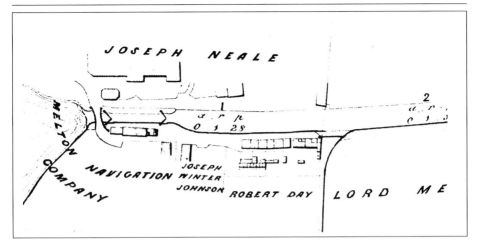

The wharf at Melton Mowbray. Detail from the plan drawn by Stephen Fry (post–1849) for the Midland Railway. (See p. 15 of part one.)

The ford and stone bridge leading to the level crossing on Burton Street in 1890. A photograph of the crossing gates is on p. 22.

OAKHAM NAVIGATION.

RECEIVED the *31st.* day of *March* 180*4*
of Mr. *Rich^d. Day Twentyfive*
Pounds, being *Twentyfive* per Cent on *One*
Shares in the intended Canal from MELTON MOW-
BRAY to OAKHAM

29.	£.	s.	d,
23.	95	0	0
24th.			
25.			
26.			

Robt. Hawley

making
£130..0..0 app^l.   } *Treasurer.*

Clementson, Printer, Melton,

Interest — 3 - 11 - 5

A receipt for the final instalment on one share in the Melton to Oakham Canal Company,
issued to Richard Day of Wymondham for share No. 183 after his death!

Burton Street in the great flood of 1908.

A horse being led to safety
from one of the stables off
Burton Street in the
disastrous flood of 1899.

Burton Street 'Top End', showing Lamberts Lane, the narrow street that connected Burton Street with Sherrard Street before the First World War. Mr Francis Wallin is driving out of Lamberts Lane.

Spectators walking to Burton Races along Burton Street, *c.* 1900.

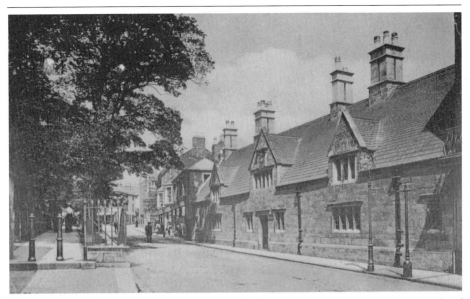

The Bede House Library and Museum in 1904. Originally built to house poor people of the town in 1646 as a result of a gift by Robert Hudson in 1638, the building was converted into a museum in 1847 by Mr W. Latham and Mr J. Woodcock.

Melton Carnival, 25 June 1925. This was the leading float on Burton Street, before it was conveyed around the town. The carnival queen Miss F. Caparn is seated in the centre. Left to right: Miss B. Rice, Miss Holmes, Maurice Ennalls, Jean Ennalls, Miss P. Southerington, Miss M. Wallin, –?–. See p. 69.

Nurses from the War Memorial Hospital with a barrel organ collecting cash for the Melton Hospital fête, June 1936. They are outside the Bede Houses on Burton Street.

Burton Street, 1928.

Anne of Cleves House/the Old Rectory (now a restaurant), Burton Street in 1904.

A view of the town in 1911 showing the Burton Street bridge on the left.

Burton Street, 1904. The Colles Hall built in 1890 to the memory of the Revd W.M. Colles is on the left, while the Crown public house is on the right. The licensee was Henry Biddles.

A general view of Burton Street, c. 1928. Note the petrol pumps in front of the Melton Garage, built into the pavement.

Burton Street, *c*. 1950.

An advertisement dating from the 1940s.

Sutton Bros butchers, Burton Street, 1936.

The Melton Garage, Burton Street, 1936.

The Boat Inn and Toad Hall, Burton Street, 1965.

Birmingham Row off Burton Street, 1965. These houses were built for canal workers employed on the Melton and Oakham Navigations in around 1800, and were demolished in the 1970s.

The Midland Railway station, 1910.

The level crossing, Burton Street, 1895.

Sidings and storage area outside the Midland Railway station, 1967.

An extension to the sidings shown in the photograph above, and the junction with the main line.

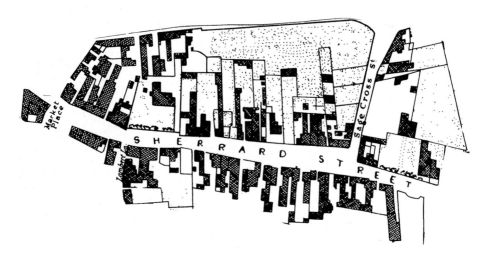

Sherrard Street, *c*. 1840.

Sherrard Street in the winter of 1880. The horse drawn cab stands opposite the entrance to Lamberts Lane.

The Marquis of Granby public house on Sherrard Street, 1910. Edward Cragg was the licensee. The Whitsuntide parade is passing by, being led by the town band, on its way to Thorpe End.

Sherrard Street, *c.* 1908. The tree on the left stands in the grounds of The Limes and is opposite Lamberts Lane, which leads to Burton Street. The photographer was standing in the Market Place.

Sherrard Street looking towards Thorpe End, 1908. The photographer stood opposite Lamberts Lane, and the boundary wall to The Limes is on the left.

A view of the Market Place, c. 1920. Lamberts Lane is on the left and has been widened. The trees in the grounds of The Limes had certainly become overgrown. It is hard to believe that Woolworths now stands on the site of this house.

The Black Swan ('Mucky Duck') public house (licensee George Robinson) on the right, with the Old Bishop Blaize public house (licensee John Thomas Smith) opposite, 1920.

EMILIE BULL

Millinery and Robes of Distinction

29 Sherrard Street, MELTON MOWBRAY

A typical 1920s advertisement, printed on a paper bag.

Albert Edward Grimbley, brush manufacturer, standing in the doorway to his shop, 10 Sherrard Street, 1908.

The street market on Sherrard Street in the 1920s. The Variety Stores stands on the corner of Windsor Street.

Belvoir Hunt leaving the Market Place, 1950. It is passing Sharman and Ladbury's garage.

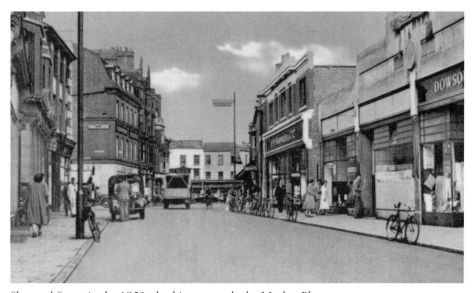

Sherrard Street in the 1950s, looking towards the Market Place.

Part of Sharman and Ladbury's garage staff, 1948. Left to right: J. Stevens, A. Charles, W. Cheshire, H. Wright, G. Ames, H. Barratt. The photograph was taken at the rear of the garage in Elms Road.

Mr F.A. Payne and Miss I. Bodycote, Sales Manager and Secretary of Sharman and Ladbury, 1937.

Harpers Cycle Co. Ltd, 47 Sherrard Street, 1937. Six cycles are displayed on the pavement.

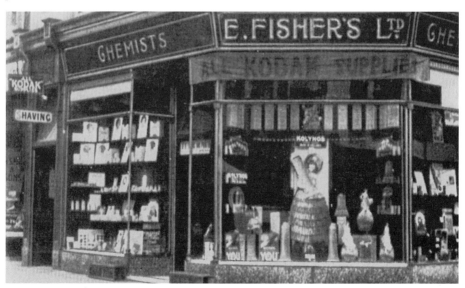

E. Fisher, chemist, 2 Sherrard Street, 1937. The shop was on the corner with Burton Street.

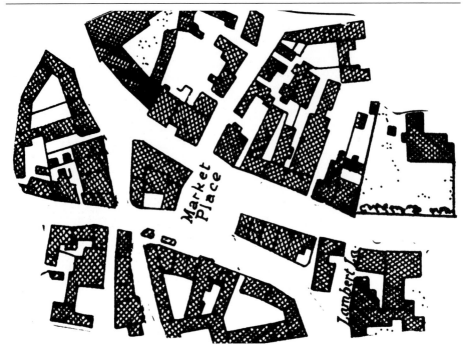

A plan of the Market Place in the middle of the nineteenth century, showing the surrounding streets and lanes.

The centre of Melton Mowbray, showing the Tuesday market, 1892. The photograph was taken from the battlements of St Mary's church.

Belvoir Hunt and hounds in the Market Place, 1936.

The Marquis of Waterford and his gang painting the White Swan red. Many historians consider that this is how the phrase 'painting the town red' originated. The incident was a result of consuming too much wine at the Croxton Park races on 6 April 1837.

Cheese Fair, 1904. In the background to the left is Towne & Co., stationer and printer, 28 Market Place. Harry Holmes was proprietor. In the centre stands Wing and Son, grocer and chemist, 29 Market Place – now the premises of W.H. Smith, stationer and bookseller.

The Market Place, 1908.

A halfpenny issued in Melton Mowbray in 1666 by Roger Waite, a local trader. The shortage of coins of the realm owing to the Civil War resulted in thousands of local trading tokens being issued throughout the country. This of course gave a monopoly of business to the person issuing the tokens, as his coin could only be spent in his own trading establishment.

Melton Mowbray is the centre for the marketing of Stilton cheese, which gets its name from the village of Stilton on the Great North Road in Cambridgeshire. This old print was published on a cigarette card by Hignetts in 1925. Stilton probably originated in a farm house dairy at Wymondham to be developed by monks at Kirby Bellars priory, two miles to the south-west of Melton Mowbray, in the sixteenth century. For further information consult *The History of Stilton Cheese.*

The Market Place, 1915. Left to right: William Barnes & Co., general and fancy draper, milliner, dress and mantle maker, outfitter and gentlemen's mercer, 20 Market Place; Pearks Stores, grocer; J. Towne & Co., stationer, printer, dealer in fancy goods and toys and circulating library.

Market Place viewed from Sherrard Street, with the 'Barnes block' centre background, 1920.

Melton Mowbray horse parade, 1910.

The Market Place laid out for the street party that celebrated the coronation of King George VI, 1937. Warners Café and fruiterers, 6 and 7 Market Place, is shown.

A 1940s advertisement for a café that was 'Mecca' for visiting villagers to the market town in the dark days of the Second World War.

A dramatic photograph taken at night of the Swan porch, 1967.

A view from the first floor window of W.H. Smith, looking into the market square, early 1950s.

W. E. Warner Limited

MARKET STORES

Melton Mowbray

R.A.C. RESTAURANT

PARTIES CATERED FOR

CONFECTIONERS

PORK PIE MANUFACTURERS

Telephone: 33 (Private Branch Exchange)

Telegrams: "KEENKUT" Melton

A 1940s advertisement for a splendid restaurant to the left of the photograph above, where the compiler of this collection spent many happy hours on market days in his youth. It is now the home of Thomas Cook, travel agent.

Barnes, Pearks, Towns and The Public Boot Benefit Company in 1916.

The Market Place, 1936.

Tuesday market, 1936.

Cheapside and South Parade viewed from the Market Place, c. 1969. The 'Barnes block' had been demolished by this time.

The famous Swan porch after the disastrous fire of 18 September 1985. The Grapes public house is on the right. Shortly after this photograph was taken the whole of the porch collapsed, but the blackened white swan was rescued and cleaned. In the cleaning process all the red paint daubed on by the Marquis of Waterford in 1837 was finally removed. The porch has been rebuilt but now stands on classical stone columns!

Belvoir Hunt accepting a stirrup cup from Warners Café in front of W.H. Smith, *c.* 1950.

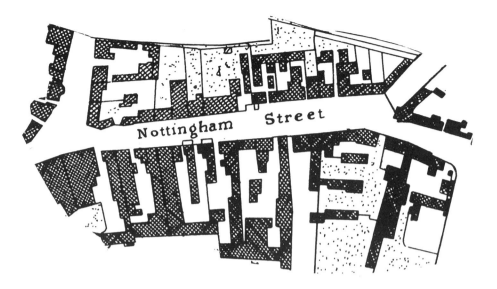

A plan of Nottingham Street in the middle of the nineteenth century.

The Baptist chapel with the King's Head Inn on the left in the 1890s.

Revd W.G. Anderson officiated at the Baptist chapel in Nottingham Street in 1934. He was a missionary in Africa from 1892 until 1900.

The Cottesmore Hunt Ale.

GREEN & JOHNSON,

BREWERS, WHISSENDINE.

NOTED ALES AND STOUT.

Melton Mowbray Office, Nottingham Street.

An 1890s advertisement for a famous hunting ale brewed in Whissendine, which was sold on Nottingham Street, Melton Mowbray.

The Bell Hotel on Nottingham Street, and looking towards Cheapside, South Parade and the Market Place, 1900. The crossroads at this point was Cornhill, and the lamppost occupies the site of the old Corn Cross.

Nottingham Street, 1904. The Eight Bells public house is on the right, where the licensee was William Wood.

The Old Kings Head (licensee Rice Cameron), 1920, before the extensive modernization programme.

Barclays Bank and the Bell Hotel, 1936.

E. Hollingshead, 27 and 28 Nottingham Street, saddler and manufacturer of hunting equipment, 1937.

W.H. Houghton & Co., 15 Nottingham Street, 1937. The shop was agent for BSA, Triumph, Norton, Sunbeam, OK Supreme and Royal Enfield motor cycles, pedal cycles and tandems.

Sharpe's Stores,
hardware dealer, 10
and 11 Nottingham
Street, 1937.

Sharpe's Stores delivery van on Scalford Road, c. 1920, loaded ready for a run in the local countryside. Sharpe's made a weekly delivery of paraffin and other essential commodities to outlying villages, hamlets, farms and houses.

A 'Bull Nose' Morris stands outside the Bell Hotel, where A.E. Wemyss was the proprietor, 1936. Boots the Chemist is on the left in South Parade. Leonard Gill, ironmongers, is situated in the 'Barnes block' in the middle distance.

Skinner and Rook, wine and spirit merchants, 37 Nottingham Street, 1937. The manager was T.R. Knight.

A pre-Second World War advertisement for one of Melton Mowbray's famous pork pie manufacturers.

The Corn Exchange, with Dickinson and Morris next door, 1936.

The Duke and Duchess of Gloucester attending the British Legion Ball at the Corn Exchange, 1936. They resided at Warwick Lodge during the hunting season.

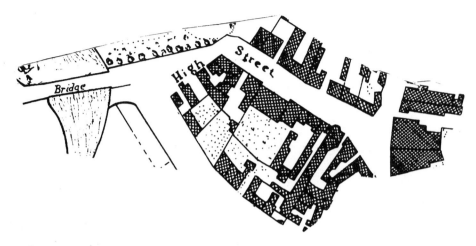

High Street in the nineteenth century, long before Wilton Road was built.

High Street, 1906. The photograph was taken by W. Till of 19 and 20 Burton Street, photographer and picture framer.

A painting by John Ferneley of Mr G. Petre's coach leaving the George Hotel on High Street, 1818.

The George Hotel, 1916. Henry William Sampey was the manager. In the centre background is the Bell Hotel, where Miss Mary Hammond was proprietress.

J. ATTENBURROW

M.P.S.   PHARMACIST

DISPENSING AND

AGRICULTURAL CHEMIST

PERFUMES AND

TOILET   REQUISITES

1 HIGH   STREET,
MELTON MOWBRAY
Telephone: 84

Advertisement for Attenburrow's chemist, with a photograph of the owner Mr James Attenburrow, 1937.

Photograph of Dr Montague Dixon MD and the White House, High Street, his home, 1902.

Garners Garage, 1936. It was on the corner of High Street and Wilton Road.

Mr G.H. Pidgeon and Mr J. Elliot, Sales Manager and Service Manager respectively, of Garner and Sons, 1937.

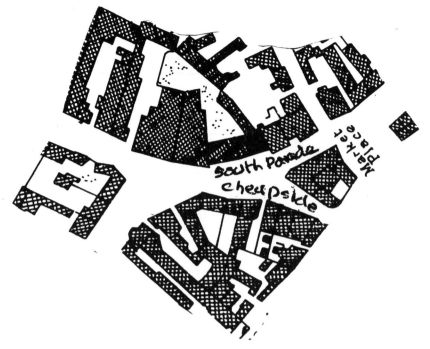

Plan of South Parade and Cheapside in the middle of the nineteenth century.

South Parade, leading to Nottingham Street, and Cheapside, leading to High Street, 1885. The thatched cottage in the centre background faced Corn Hill. It was demolished in 1897.

South Parade, 1890.

J.W. Warners, printer, bookbinder, publisher, bookseller, stationer and circulating library, 2 South Parade, 1904.

Postcard forwarded to Mrs A.H. Marsh from the Holgate Boot Co. The card was printed by Warners of 2 South Parade and posted in 1908.

Tylers of 3 South Parade, 1937. They had taken over the premises of the Holgate Boot Co.

W. A. HEAP,

𝔚𝔦𝔫𝔢 & 𝔖𝔭𝔦𝔯𝔦𝔱 TRADE 🦌 MARK. 𝔐𝔢𝔯𝔠𝔥𝔞𝔫𝔱,

MANUFACTURER OF THE CELEBRATED

PURE MINERAL WATERS AND LEMONADE,

PREPARED ONLY WITH FILTERED SPRING WATER,

KING STREET HOUSE AND CHEAPSIDE,

MELTON MOWBRAY.

Lemonade and Soda Water supplied in the Patent Syphon specially adapted for Invalids.

Advertisement published in the 1890s. William Albert Heap brewed beer on his premises in King Street, retailing it on Cheapside.

The Cheapside of the 'Barnes block', 1880s. Note the town pump in front of S. Manchester's, general furnisher.

W. Easom, grocer, commenced business in 1790 and traded through the reigns of eleven monarchs, closing down in the 1960s.

Garners on Cheapside, 1937. The shop was established in 1740.

Cheapside, looking towards South Parade, *c*. 1905.

W. Bowley and Co., proprietor W.E. Katz, jeweller, silversmith and optician on the corner of Cheapside in the 'Barnes block', 1936.

Brownlow, chemist and druggist, 6 Cheapside, 1926.

Cheapside on the right, South Parade on the left, and the 'Barnes block' in the centre, 1936.

Three Tuns public house, 3 King Street, 1912. John Meadows was the publican.

M. Bull, farrier for fox hunters, in his forge off King Street, 1911.

Jacob Brotherhood's travelling horse drawn van in 1916. His shop was at 53 and 54 King Street.

The Plaza cinema, King Street. Built in 1918, it was converted to a bingo hall in the 1950s, and demolished in July 1982 as part of a road improvement scheme.

Two horse drawn vans loaded ready for trading in the surrounding villages. Picks Stores was situated at 1 Kings Road.

Aerial view of Kings Road, 1933, showing the Midland Woodworking Company and the Snow Hill brick pits.

The Golden Fleece public house, 1891. John Simpson was publican.

C.B. Payne's furniture shop on the corner of Park Lane, 1 Leicester Street, 1905.

The grocer's shop of Miss Mary Ann Allen, 1898, standing on the corner of Timber Hill and Sage Cross Street. It was adjacent to the imposing structure of the Wesleyan chapel, where the ministers were the Revd Robert Daw and the Revd Ralph Calderbank.

The Round Houses, Sage Cross Street, built in the grounds of The Limes towards the end of the eighteenth cuntury at the expense of the Stokes family, and occupied by three maiden sisters. The houses, octagonal in shape, contained three rooms, and the gardens where the same size as each house. They were unique, and when this photograph was taken in 1911 they were considered to be of considerable architectural importance. The houses were wantonly demolished in 1980 to make way for a doctor's surgery.

The tollgate that stood at the junction of Thorpe Road and Saxby Road on Thorpe End in 1837, when the Marquis of Waterford with his unruly crew painted the gates and the keeper's cottage red. See p. 33.

Thorpe End viewed from Sherrard Street, 1904. The Marquis of Granby public house is on the right; Edward Cragg was publican. Thomas Moore's bakehouse, 1 Thorpe End, stands centre left. It has been long since demolished in a road widening scheme.

Carnegie Library on Thorpe End, photographed shortly after it was opened in 1904. Mr Andrew Carnegie donated £2,000 towards the construction of the building on land donated by the town estate. It is now the tourist centre and museum.

The start of the Melton Carnival parade outside the Carnegie Library, 25 June 1925.

The Wheatsheaf public house, Thorpe End, demolished as part of a road improvement scheme on 28 December 1983.

Thorpe Road, 1904. On the right is the entrance to Stafford Avenue. Thorpe Road post office stands on the corner. John Thomas Bilson was the post office clerk.

Leicester Road bridge, 1903.

Leicester Road, 1905. Egerton Park is on the left, open fields on the right. These are now the Town Estate recreation park and tennis courts.

Carson's Garage, owned by Mr Peter Weaver, 1936.

St Mary's church morning Sunday School class, 1934, with Miss Margaret Sansby.

The junction of Nottingham Road, Asfordby Road and Park Road, now Norman Way. See also p. 77.

Nottingham Road, *c.* 1920. The entrance to the Crescent is on the left of the photograph.

A painting by Claude Ferneley of his father, John, working in his studio at Elgin Lodge, Scalford Road, *c.* 1825.

A Class B1 in full steam leaving the Melton Northern station bound for Skegness, *c.* 1940. The cantilever signal box on the left of the photograph was to a London & North Western Railway design, and swayed in high winds!

Entrance to the refreshment rooms and toilets on the Northern station, *c.* 1950.

The entrance to the refreshment room when the railway station on Scalford Road was being demolished, 1967. A fine example of terracotta work was lost forever.

The last days of a magnificent railway station, 1967.

London & North Eastern Railway bridge crossing Scalford Road, 1969.

Entrance to Cottesmore Avenue on Asfordby Road, 1930.

Traffic island on the Asfordby Road, Nottingham Road, Park Road and Wilton Road junction, *c.* 1950.

Shouler's saleroom on Norman Street, demolished in the building of the relief road Norman Way in the 1980s.

The last day. Miss Cicely Maycock, headmistress (with basket), saying goodbye to all her children on the day that St Mary's Norman Street Church of England Infants School closed for the last time, 1 July 1977.

Entrance to the War Memorial Hospital on Ankle Hill, 1928. The memorial to the left of the gateway has been removed since this photograph was taken.

Dalby Road near the junction with Leicester Road, 1926. The swimming baths now occupy the overgrown area to the right of the photograph.

Dalby Road, looking down the hill, *c.* 1905. Ankle Hill is to the right of the photograph.

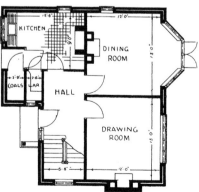

Green Acre, The Drive, Dalby Road, built by E. Clarke and Sons for Mr W. Bailes in the early 1930s for £850. This is one of the quality houses built by Clarkes in Melton Mowbray on the Dalby Road estate before the Second World War.

Section Two
STATELY RESIDENCES

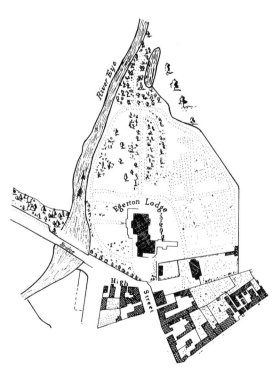

Plan of Egerton Lodge, c. 1840. Wilton Road had yet to be built.

Egerton Lodge, 1903, before the extensive demolition of part of this historic house.

Mr Arthur Vickris Pryor DL, JP, who resided at Egerton Lodge when the photograph above was taken. Mr Pryor was educated at Eton, was a Justice of the Peace, and hunted with the Quorn, Belvoir and Cottesmore hounds; he was Deputy Lieutenant for Leicestershire and married Elizabeth Countess of Wilton, the owner of Egerton Lodge, in 1886. See p. 153.

Melton Mowbray Urban District Council, photographed at the grand opening of Melton Mowbray Town Hall, Egerton Lodge, on 10 October 1929. Front row, left to right: J. Sparling, H.C. Holmes, T. Brown, R.W. Brownlow, W. Greaves, O. Brotherhood, G.H. Hinman. Back row: E. Steans, C.S. Jenkins, G.W. Goodacre, W.H. Jarvis (surveyor and engineer), H.K. Barker (clerk), E.D. Hayes, F.R. Bailey, G.W. Selby.

The Town Hall and Gardens, Egerton Lodge, 1936.

Woodville, a charming house, 65 Burton Street, 1962. This was built in 1837 for Joseph Neale, surveyor to the Oakham Canal Company navigation system.

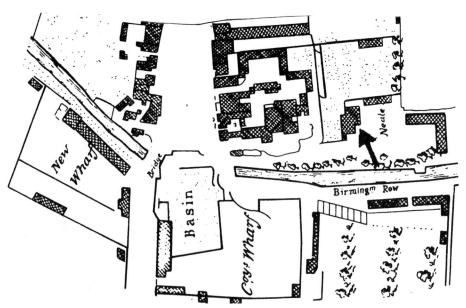

Plan of the basin and surrounding area drawn two years after Woodville was built. The house is indicated with an arrow. The bay window on the left was added later. An important building, part of our industrial heritage, it was demolished by Pedigree Petfoods in the early 1980s.

Newport Lodge was built in 1849. The Earl of Bradford made extensive alterations, converting the house to a fine hunting lodge. It is seen here in 1903.

Captain Robert Bunten Muir in residence at Newport Lodge, 1903. He held the rank of Major in the Leicestershire Yeomanry and was Captain of the 65th Squadron, 17th Battalion in the Boer War for thirteen months. Captain Muir hunted with all three local packs of hounds.

The Limes, 1903. It is hard to imagine that the shops in the centre of Melton Mowbray now occupy the site of this splendid house. A tragic loss of an historic and architecturally important building.

Mr James Pacey JP, the owner of The Limes when the photograph above was taken. He purchased the property in 1889 for £3,000. Mr Pacey was born at Garthorpe in 1846 and at the time this photograph was taken in 1903 was a partner in the local brewery, Adcock, Pacey and Company, brewers of fine beer.

Hamilton Lodge was built in 1902 by Gavin, 2nd Lord Hamilton of Dalzell, KCVO. Frances, Countess of Warwick purchased the house a few years later and renamed it Warwick Lodge. The Duke and Duchess of Gloucester rented the property in 1935 for a number of seasons. In 1955 the house was purchased by the Melton and Belvoir Rural District Council for use as their offices and council chambers.

Melton and Belvoir RDC, at Warwick Lodge, May 1961. Back row, left to right: D. Headly, Revd R.T. Seivewright, A. Livingstone, E.W. Green, S.W. Birch, H.E. Hickling, R.W. Toon, G. Abbott, D.F. Sanday, S.S. Exton, L.E. Jesson. Centre row, left to right: H.L. Brown, G.E. Dalton, F.T. Whait, W.R. Allwood, H. Lord, S.W. Warrington, W. Miller, H.D. Hornsby, H. Smith, S.A. Eggleston, P.F. Dalton, L. Thacker, G.M. Hutchinson, J.K. Hart, G.H. Houghton, D. Babbington-Smith. Front row, left to right: T. Thurman, Mrs P.E. Garratt, Mrs M.B. Lee, W.E. Stanley, J.G. Burgin, A.P. Marsh (clerk), P.R. Hill (chairman), J.F. Groome (vice chairman), W.T. Orson, Mrs M.L. Aspell, Mrs L.R. Croome, H.A. Lewis (treasurer), J.P. Milburn (surveyor).

Colonel Charles Wyndham purchased Hill House on Ankle Hill in the early 1840s, then proceeded to build a house, seen here in 1906, that he named Wyndham Lodge. Colonel Wyndham had an exciting army career, serving with the Scots Greys in the Peninsular War, and fighting with Wellington at Waterloo.

War Memorial Hospital, Melton Mowbray, Wyndham Lodge. In August 1920 Colonel Richard Dalgleish agreed to purchase Wyndham Lodge and 15 acres of land for converting to a hospital for £5,000 and also pay for the necessary alterations amounting to £2,000. The property was to be used as a cottage hospital in perpetuity in memory of the local lads who had died in the First World War. It was opened on 19 January 1922. See p. 79.

This house, seen here in 1912, was built in 1870 by Mr Thomas Hickson at a cost of £2,986 10s, and was named Staveley Lodge after Christopher Staveley, the local architect who designed many fine buildings in Melton Mowbray. During the Second World War it was the headquarters of a Parachute Brigade who dropped behind enemy lines at Arnhem. After the war it became the main offices for the Production Engineering Research Association (PERA).

The laboratories, workshops and offices of PERA at Staveley Lodge being overshadowed by a crane, during the construction of the Melton Mowbray Borough Council Offices on Nottingham Road.

Craven Lodge, seen here *c*. 1910, was built in 1827 by Dr Keal and called Burton House. It was purchased in 1856 by the Hon. W.G. Craven, who made extensive alterations and re-named the house.

In 1922 Craven Lodge was purchased by Captain Michael Wardell, who divided the house into several fine apartments to be let to the hunting fraternity. In 1923 the Prince of Wales took one of the apartments, and this photograph taken in 1925 shows the wing of the house that he occupied.

The Prince of Wales was a frequent visitor to Craven Lodge from 1923 to 1929, and hunted with all the local packs of hounds. This photograph taken in 1935 shows the Prince at the races with Mrs Simpson, whom he first met at Burrough Court, Burrough-on-the-Hill, a few miles to the south-east of Melton Mowbray.

In 1793 this property was called Norman House. Later it became The House, and when this photograph was taken in 1903 it was called The Elms, so named by Lieutenant Colonel William Thomas Markham who purchased the property in 1867. The house was acquired by Dr and Mrs Lionel Powell in 1893. On the death of Dr Powell in 1930 the house became derelict, and was pulled down.

The Second World War intervened and the site of The Elms was a vacant lot containing rubble and crumbling walls for many years. In 1958 a modern telephone exchange was constructed here, finally replacing the ornamental garden and magnificent house that stood for over 150 years in the centre of Melton Mowbray.

Section Three
INDUSTRY AND
COMMERCE

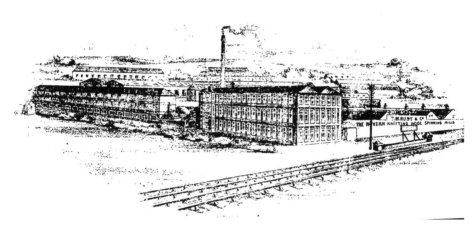

A late nineteenth-century factory, T.W. Rust and Company's Spinning Mill. It was on the site of Pedigree Petfoods food processing plant.

Enoch Evans with some of his employees standing outside his factory on Thorpe End. This photograph was taken in the 1890s. Messrs Evans and Co. was the first factory to manufacture commercially large quantities of pork pies, commencing in 1830.

An advertisement for Evans's hand raised pork pies, 1940s. Note the telephone number 5: no problems with six figure STD numbers when that telephone was installed!

Flo Stevens and helpers pour the liquid jelly into Melton Mowbray pork pies.

John Crosher shows John Greenslade and a party of schoolboys how Stilton cheese is made, 1947.

An advertisement, 1940s. Stilton cheese could only be produced under licence as it was considered a luxury, which was not necessary to sustain the war effort.

Eddy Fryer tips the local farmers' milk into the weigh bowl.

Harry Searle operates the milk pasteurizer.

Linda Hammond pierces Stilton cheese to enable the famous blue mould to form.

Jim Mayfield, head cheesemaker, on the left of the photograph, assists in cutting the Leicester cheese curd.

E. Clarke and Sons and the Midlands Woodworking Co. on Kings Road, Melton Mowbray shared a number of facilities on the factory site during their early years. This photograph of 1925 shows the first three ladies to be employed in the combined works at the entrance to the shared office. Standing, left to right: Miss Ena Goodacre, Miss Janet Marchent (the first lady employees of the Midland Wordworking Co.). Seated: Miss Olive Rowell (the first lady to be employed by E. Clarke and Sons).

Midland Woodworking lorry standing outside Snow Hill Garage, *c.* 1935. The garage was a subsidiary of the Midland Woodworking Co.

Outside Snow Hill Garage, 1933. Left to right: Fred Terry, Vic Bennett, –?–, Fred Gaunt, E. Glitheroe.

Edward Portess in front of Snow Hill Garage with his dog Spot, 1947.

One of the many joint projects that were entered into between E. Clarke and Sons and the Midland Woodworking Co. was constructing the horse operating theatre for the Royal Army Veterinary Corps, Welby Lane, Melton Mowbray. Left to right: Gordon Hart, Phillip Chittenden.

Printing the *Times* on the hand fed Wharfedale Press, 1911.

Mr J. Meadows working the linotype machine, 1936.

Setting type by hand in the composing room, 1936. The head of the department, Mr J. Burman, 'standing at his case', is on the left.

The first days! Don Harrison and his team tearing down part of the Paton and Baldwin factory in April 1951, before Chappie Ltd set up business.

The first retort arrives at Melton Mowbray, 1951. Chappie Ltd starts production.

The first load of petfood being dispatched from Chappie Ltd, 1952.

Chappie apprentices, March 1955. Left to right: P. Taft, R. Dyckhoff, A. Lawson, J. Gaunt (head of training), M. Yapp, W. Sawicki, J. French.

The first poster issued by Chappie Ltd, to be posted on hoardings on selected sites around the country in May 1955. The company also considered going into films at this time, featuring Miss Kit-E-Kat and her family, as part of their advertising programme.

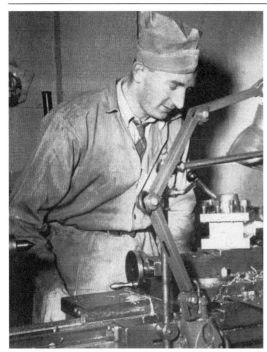

Ron Acton, a member of the Red Shift maintenance crew, working his lathe, May 1955.

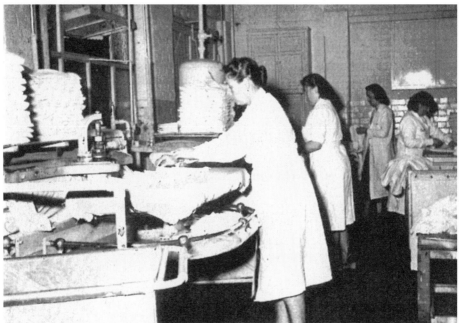

Chappie Ltd laundry, July 1955. It processed 16,000 garments per week. The manager of this unit was Mr E.W. Langford.

Bridging the Scalford brook, September 1955.

A few months later. The new bridge serving the factory exit in 1956.

The first traffic lights to be permanently erected in Melton Mowbray, November 1955. They were to control the flow of traffic from Chappie Ltd on to Mill Street.

The four catering supervisors, November 1957. Left to right: Miss K. Doyle, Mrs D. Hyde, Mrs A. Wildon, Mrs G. Degg.

Mrs Phyllis Miller (née Welbourn) of Wymondham distributing light refreshments in the canteen, July 1955. Mrs Miller was born in Wymondham in 1918, served in the RAF during the Second World War as an administrative NCO, and joined Chappie Ltd in 1953.

Factory scenes, 1955. Top left: Arthur Hubbard filling the retorts using an overhead gantry. Top right: Mr K. Polec unloading tins in the goods-in department. The conveyor in the foreground delivered the cans to the filling station. Bottom left: Dennis Atkinson driving his 'stacatruc'. Bottom right: a new innovation for the food preparation department in 1955 was the installation of a Wetter bandsaw for cutting up frozen blocks of meat. Mr John Paszynski is seen operating it.

Ron Hurd working the labelling machine, January 1956. Ron worked for Paton and Baldwin, and was one of the first people to join Chappie Ltd when they took over the site in 1951.

Roof maintenance by the permanent maintenance team, July 1956. Left to right: Reg Marshall, Gordon Hack, George Davie.

A battery of retorts in full steam, 1956.

Jack Bonshor operating a can unscrambler in September 1956. Jack, a keen local cricketer, played for Egerton Park, averaging thirty-two runs per innings during the 1954 season.

New recruits to the office training scheme, September 1956. Left to right: Miss Anne Payne, Miss Pamela Hopkins, Miss Jane Ball, Miss Joan Lester.

Mr G. Southerington maintaining a steady head of steam in the boiler room, April 1957. Mr Southerington served in the Royal Artillery Signals Division during the Second World War. He took part in the Battle of Arnhem, being taken prisoner after eight days of fighting.

Sheep pens in the cattle market off Scalford Road, 1950.

Fatstock pens, 1968, the year in which the grand re-opening by the Rt. Hon. Cledwyn Hughes MP took place.

Section Four
EDUCATION, RECREATION AND PASTIMES

An engraving of St. Mary's Church in 1879 by Claude Ferneley.

Children in the Play Close, 1902.

Sheep grazing in the Play Close, 1904.

The Play Close, *c*. 1910.

The entrance to the Play Close and Town Park on Leicester Street was improved by the Town Estate in 1907 and 1909, when the town wardens were Henry Wood and R.W. Brownlow.

Children's bathing pool in the Play Close, 1936. This popular pool has long since been removed, in the cause of good hygiene.

Ladies relaxing on the grass in front of the bandstand in the park, *c.* 1925.

The 'landing stage' and steps down to the River Eye just before the First World War, when rowing on the river was a pleasant Sunday afternoon pastime.

Rowing on the River Eye to the west of Egerton Park, *c.* 1910.

Two moored rowing boats and a dinghy in full sail on the River Wreake near Sysonby church, before the First World War.

The 'duck raft' in front of Egerton Lodge when it was still the Council Offices. These rafts were maintained at the expense of Mr Joseph Hill with the permission of the Borough Council.

The street party on Nottingham Street to celebrate Queen Elizabeth II's Silver Jubilee, 6 June 1977.

A decorated lorry, part of Queen Elizabeth II's Silver Jubilee celebrations, leaving Thorpe End for Sherrard Street, 7 June 1977. It is passing Parke House Garage with the Wesleyan chapel high in the background. Both these buildings have now been demolished.

Melton Rovers in the cul-de-sac next to Beeby's Yard off Burton Street, 1918–19 season. On the end of the second row, right, sit Gildone and Sleath, with Jack Hazelwood sitting on the extreme left of the front row.

Representative side from Melton Mowbray and district schools, 1928–9 season. Back row, left to right: John Moore, Len Harker, Frank Harding, Walter Harris, John Bilby, Dagger Ward. Front row: Jack Williams, George Parr, John Bateson, Arthur Core, Cecil Muse.

The top class football team of the 1944–5 season that represented the RAF at Melton Mowbray. Back row, left to right: Andy Bromley, Bill Maclean, –?–, Flight Lieutenant Ames. Centre row: –?–, Alan Brown, Ted Sale, –?–, McKie, Oswald Destine, Roy Bentley. Front row: Clem Stevenson, Jimmy Learmonth, Fred Moon, Group Captain Gomez, Bert Brocklehurst, Fred Butcher, Jack Smith. Bill Maclean was the trainer for Leicester City Football Club before and after the Second World War.

Melton Town Football Club, 1948–9 season. Back row, left to right: George Calwell, Joe Eglestone, Dixie McNeil, Jack Rodgers, Arthur Core, Fred Parr. Front row: Haden Hicks, Jimmy Learmonth, Les Staff, Billy Caithness, Vic Orridge.

Leicestershire playing Somerset at Egerton Park, Melton Mowbray in the summer of 1946.

Eddie Dawson of Sycamore House, Wymondham, 1934. He captained Leicestershire for four seasons between 1928 and 1933, and played for England in South Africa. Dawson was considered to be one of the finest batsmen who played for Cambridge before the Second World War.

Thorpe Arnold Cricket Club, 1931. Back row, left to right: I. Brown, S. Elsom, W. Smith, O. Lockton, H. Parkes, W. Hodgkinson. Front row: N. Tyrell, G. Fleckney, F. Hodgkinson, L. Perkins, S. Wyles.

Brian Keightley and Dennis Parr going out to bat on the Thorpe Arnold cricket ground, Thorpe Road, Melton Mowbray, 1965. Mrs Pearson and Michael are in the background.

Melton Town Ladies' Bowling Club, 1952, in front of the pavilion off Saxby Road. Standing on the steps of the pavilion, left to right: Mrs M. Portess, Miss E. Sharpe. Standing: Mrs Baxter, –?–, Mrs Fitzgerald, –?–, Mrs Sansby, Edith Plumb, Mrs Irons, Mrs Lister, Mrs Bissell, Eadie Payne, Anne Hibbert. Seated: Ester Barry, Mrs Plumb, Mrs Barton, Mrs Whitbread, Mrs Wormleighton, Mrs Chapman, Mrs Mee. Seated on the grass: Hilary Portess, Pamela Clamp.

Melton Town Gentlemen's Bowling Club, 1951. Standing, left to right: H. Cliff, C. Wesson, P. Lisle, –?–, C. Skinner, N. Brooks, C. Mayo, J. Barton, C. Pick, G. Payne, J. Williams, R. Arnold. Seated: E. Fitzgerald, R. Watts, H. Smith, P. Challis.

The observation post for the war-time observer corps was situated in a field behind Melbray Drive, off Scalford Road. Back row, left to right: Jack Brydges, ? Tuneley, Tom Golling, Hedley Clift, Ernie Bartram, Sid Saul, Frank Sanders, Stan Leach. Middle row: Edward Portess, Steve North, Joe Morrison, Jack Golling, Charlie Walkden, Claude Hill. Front row: Rex Polendine, Bernard Turner, ? Lunn, Gordon Astill, Jess Tinkler, Tom Barnard.

Jess Tinkler, motor engineer and part-time observer in the Second World War. Before the D-Day landings Jess Tinkler, Rex Polendine and Joe Morrison were recruited as volunteers to assist in the landings on the Normandy beaches. This was a highly secretive mission. Business associates, family and friends did not know that these three were at sea on a variety of ships, acting as observers for the invading allied forces. This was particularly awkward for Jess who was employed in a local garage. Rex and Joe were full-time observers, but Jess's absence as head of the service department for three months without any communication alienated his employers, who sacked him in his absence. On returning home this brave man found he had no job to go to. A fine thank you! Eventually he set up his own garage in Mill Street.

Wesleyan Band, *c.* 1920.

Melton Town Silver Prize Band, 1937. The conductor was Mr H.V. Dyson. Back row, left to right: Frank Hurd, Cyril Walker, Bill Guilford, John Way, Frank Handley, Vic Richardson, Charles Biddles, Baden Holmes, Sid Wesson. Middle row: Arthur Sisson, Arthur Bartram, Bill Hart, Arthur Slater, Harry Chatwin, Horace Handley, John Crowder, Sam Manchester, Randall Pollard, Bert Rands, Bert Page. Front row: Nobby Clarke, Charles Robinson, Frank Pollard, Whitley Brownlow, W.V. Dyson, Alfred Handley, Bill Wesson, Jack Pollard, Jack Kilby.

Melton Mowbray Operatic Society, 1930. Miss Anne Kestin and Aldith Roper in *Zurika*.

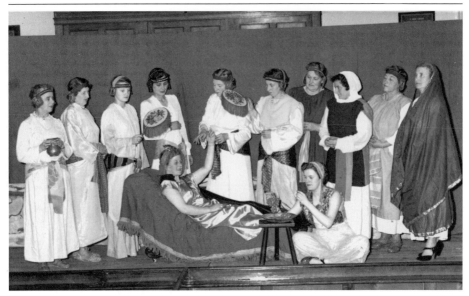

The Congregational chapel travelling concert party, *c.* 1950. This group of volunteer entertainers travelled around the villages in the Melton Mowbray area entertaining the locals in village halls and chapels.

The 'Tally Ho' band marching out of Nottingham Street into South Parade and Cheapside during the celebrations for Queen Elizabeth II's Silver Jubilee.

Melton Mowbray Cycle Club Committee, 1905. The founder of this club, Mr Harry Wesson, is seated in the front row on the left, in the light coloured jacket.

Harry and Lucy Wesson seated on the Hilda Cycle, named after their first daughter. Harry Wesson invented the Hilda Cycle, and traded from 5 Sage Cross Street. The photograph was taken on the Leicester Road, outside Egerton Park, in 1905.

The County Technical College, King Street, when it was opened in September 1937. This college was built on the site of the County Police Station built in 1842.

The first principal of the County Technical College, William Wall BSc, AIC.

The Old Police Station, King Street, built on the site of the Bridewell (prison). The Marquis of Waterford and some of his cronies spent a night in the Bridewell in April 1837, and did not think much of it!

Melton Mowbray Central Boys School, Limes Avenue, built in 1928.

HRH The Duke of Gloucester, who
officially opened the Central Boys
School on 7 December 1933.

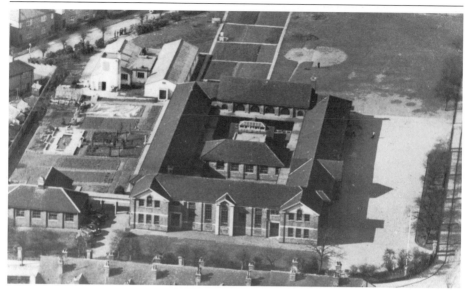

Melton Mowbray Central Boys School, 1935. It is now the Brownlow Infants School.

Teaching staff of the Central Boys School surrounded by their pupils in 1933. Staff, left to right: L. Cullen, –?–, C. Walkden, L. Till, C. Goldspink, (Nunc) Hubbard, Holt, Peabody, C. Mayo, S. (Pop) Berry.

Melton Mowbray Modern Boys School prefects, 1948. Back row, left to right: Hendey, Exton, Hickman. Front row: Hebb, McNeill, Timbrell, Henfrey, Bonser.

The Coronation Party at Kings Road Infants School, 1953.

Kitchen staff of Kings Road Infants School, 1950. Left to right: Mabel Watkin, Mrs Startin, Mrs Dalby, –?–, Mrs Isherwood.

Kings Road Infants School staff, 1924. Back row, left to right: Miss Needham, Miss Goodchild, Miss Branston, Miss E. Cox. Front row: Miss Cox, Miss Brown (headmistress), Miss White, –?–.

Kings Road Infants School staff, 1940. Back row, left to right: Miss Branston, Miss Cox, Mrs Jenner. Front row: Elspeth Cox, Mrs Bodycote, Miss Needham (headmistress), Miss Wright, Miss J. Sherwin.

King Edward VII Grammar School, Burton Road, 1933.

Miss Mawby's class at King Edward VII Grammar School, 1952. Doug Ecob is holding an ice-cream cone over the head of Miss Mawby. Also in the group are: Davina Muggleton, Pat Lightfoot, Ann Jallands, Nora Wartnaby, Janet Lunn, Jackie Ray, Jill Wallace, Rosemary Hodgson, Wendy Cartwright, Pauline Shepherd, Pam Chaplin, Brigid Newbold, Ann Breward, Joy Middleton, Gwen Starbuck, Wendy Golling, Maureen Rippon, Marjorie Crawford, Janet Ash, David Foster, Cliff Baguley, Graham Brooks, Peter Lewis, Bruce Needham, Carl Wright, Mike Smedley, Oscar Lay, Gus Hewson, Geoff Wade, Jon Simson, Ron Bailey, Mike Thompson, Tony Hinman, John Wright and Brian Burt.

R. Stuart Smith BA, 1937. He was appointed headmaster of King Edward VII Grammar School in September 1911.

The Modern School for Girls in Wilton Road, opened by HRH The Duke of Gloucester in December 1933. It is now the County Library.

Miss N.E. Renno, headmistress of the Girls' Modern School, 1936.

Miss C. Packer MA, senior mistress in charge of girls at the King Edward VII Grammar School, 1937.

Miss M. Smith, headmistress of Melton Primary Girls School, 1936.

Miss E. Burnett, principal of the Cairn Holt School, Asfordby Road, 1936.

The Sarson Secondary School for Girls, Burton Road, c. 1960. This school replaced the girls' school on Wilton Road.

Melton Working Men's Club, 1937. Back row, left to right: P. Handley, H. Dobney, E. Richardson, K. Hart, F. Gillett, E. Hopkins. Front row: A. Wilmott, W. Bishop, H. Richardson, J. Spiby, G. Gresham.

Melton Branch of the British Legion, 1937. Back row, left to right: C. Cobley, E. White, W. Dawson, A. Bodsworth, T. Fletcher, E. Heawood, M. Newham. Middle row: S.N. Jones, W. Wade, R. Peters, Major-General J. Vaughan, T. Brooks, A. Blakemore, B. Pacey. Front row: A. Rowden, H. Rands.

Jack Skinner, May 1956. Local entertainer and part-time trick cyclist, he appeared on television during the late 1940s and early 1950s.

Section Five
PERSONALITIES

Wood engraving of Anne of Cleves House, in front of St Mary's church, 1879.

The effigy of King Richard I in the Abbey church at Fontevrault. Richard Coeur de Lion visited Melton Mowbray in 1194, staying at the fortified manor house of William de Mowbray that stood on the site of St Mary's Way car park, near the Regal cinema. King Street was named after this king.

Effigy of King John. This unpopular king visited Melton Mowbray in 1208, 1209 and 1215, staying a number of days on each visit, principally to collect taxes and subdue his rebel barons – one of whom was William de Mowbray.

Richard III, who visited Melton
Mowbray on 25 September 1484, on his
way from Nottingham to Oakham.

Anne of Cleves. In 1540 King Henry VIII
gave part of the manor of Melton Mowbray
and a house that had belonged to the Melton
Priory to Anne of Cleves, on the
understanding that she retired to the country,
taking no part in court life. This she wisely
did. It is presumed she lived in Anne of
Cleves House on Burton Street. She led a
secretive life after the king had divorced her,
retaining her wealth, and her head.

HRH The Prince of Wales, later King Edward VII. This sporting prince enjoyed the good life in Melton Mowbray, maintaining a string of hunters in the town. When Stapleford Hall was put up for sale after the death of Lady Harborough, the royal prince endeavoured to purchase the estate. His mother thought it was too close to his Melton cronies and insisted that Sandringham was purchased instead. In May 1862 Sandringham became the prince's official residence, well away from Melton Mowbray. In the 1890s the east coast railway line was built, with a station at Sandringham, so the royal train had easy access to the 'flesh pots' of Melton Mowbray. See p. 94 in part one.

John Ferneley. This famous sporting painter was born at Thrussington in 1782. Ferneley purchased some land on Scalford Road in 1813, first building a studio big enough to hold a horse. See p. 74. He then built Elgin Lodge as his home, so named after the Elgin Marbles in the British Museum. For nearly fifty years he lived in this house painting some of the finest hunting pictures ever produced. His house and studio was open to allcomers, and was visited by the young bloods of the town, princes and kings. On market days in the 1840s and '50s a stroll up to Ferneley's for a glass of port was the order of the day. He died in 1860 aged 78, and was buried in Thrussington churchyard.

A painting inside St Mary's church, dating from *c.* 1828. On the front left is John Ferneley's family – John, Sally, Mary, William, Claud standing, Reuben sitting on a cushion. Mrs Sally Ferneley faces her children.

A drawing by Charles Simpson of the famous rough-rider Dick Christian on Lord Grey. Dick was born in March 1779 at Cottesmore near Oakham and died in June 1862 aged 84, living most of his life in Melton Mowbray. He was considered to be the finest horseman in England in his time. Married three times, his first wife bore him twenty children, his second only one. He took part in many steeplechases riding against the nobility of the day on equal terms. An eyewitness to the Cribb–Molineux fight at Thistleton Gap, he stated years later that 'I could hear the blows as plain as a drum beat.' This was the first defence of the heavyweight boxing championship of the world, in which Tom Cribb was the winner after eight rounds, on 28 September 1811.

The artist Sir Francis Grant on Grindal, by John Ferneley. A self taught artist, Grant first exhibited at the Royal Academy in 1834 at the age of 31, sending 'The Melton Breakfast'. On p. 18 of part one is a reproduction of the second version of this famous painting. In 1840 he showed a painting of Queen Victoria in Windsor Park in his Academy exhibition. He then became the painter of the day. Elected President of the Royal Academy in 1866, Grant was knighted by the Queen shortly afterwards.

Headstone of Sir Francis Grant's grave in St Mary's Close, off Norman Way. Sir Francis died suddenly in October 1878. His family and friends declined the honour of a burial at Westminster Abbey. Three hundred members of the Royal Academy joined the many hundreds who attended one of the most impressive funerals ever to be held in Melton Mowbray.

Sir Malcolm Sargent as a young man. He was organist and choirmaster at St Mary's church from 1914 to 1924. He is seen here in 1928.

Newsagent Mr E. Williams (height 47½ inches, weight 5 stone 6 pounds). He was a popular trader between the two world wars on the streets of Melton Mowbray.

Dick Burton VC unveiling the war memorial to the dead of the Second World War in the garden of remembrance at Egerton Lodge on 1 August 1948. Dick was educated at the Melton Modern Boys School on Limes Avenue, being awarded the VC in 1944 for action against the enemy 'way beyond the call of duty' during the Second World War.

The Countess of Wilton at a meet of the Belvoir Hunt in Egerton Park on 30 January 1914.

Senior Warden of the Town Estate in 1937, Mr S.B. Weaver.

Junior Warden of the Town Estate in 1937, Mr Len Leader.

Melton Urban District Council, 1937. Back row, left to right: C.S. Jenkins, J.G. Devitt, P.D. Prior, J. Litchfield, A.L. Sleath, H.K. Barker, W. Jarvis. Front row: T.R. Stockdale, F.R. Bailey, T. Brown, W. Greaves, H. Richardson, G.W. Selby, O. Brotherhood, S. Weaver.

Leicestershire County Council area surveyor, 1937, Captain F.C. Salmon.

Melton Urban District Council treasurer, 1937, Mr C.S. Jenkins.

Sanitary inspector for the Rural District Council, 1937, Mr A.L. Sleath.

Area surveyor for the Rural District Council, 1937, Mr L. Hesford.

Melton Urban District Council, 1949–50. Back row, left to right: E.C. Moorhouse, C.S. Jenkins, H.K. Barker, F.J. Buckmaster, W.H. Jarvis, H. Buxton, J.W. Mills, G.P. Salt. Front row: J.W. Greenslade, Mrs A.G. Marsh, E.M. Summers, S. Berry, W. Greaves, E.B. Eagles.

Presentation by Councillor Frank Buckmaster of the chain of office of Melton Urban District Council to Stanley Berry JP, Chairman 1950–1, on 23 May 1951.

Photograph of staff and Councillors to the Melton Urban District Council in front of Egerton Lodge, 1973. From back row, left to right: Paul Raymond, Bill Forkes, Mike Missett, Ted Howarth, Roy Mound, Charles Bird, Jack Martin, Walter Marshall, Tony Emmerson, Wilf Taylor, Jim Beeson, Lee Jamieson, Bryce Gommersall, Charles Bird, Mike Robinson, Jim Boyland, Charles Townend, –?–, Jack Wildman, Lesley Leng, Herman Hinchcliffe, Ray Bailey, Mrs Basford, Jack Stevenson, Dorothy Maycock, Gill Cross, Ron White, Theresa Pytlik, John Spence, Janet Hall, –?–, –?–, –?–, Joan Turner, Edith Clarke, Angela Manning, Jane Watson, Terry Larder, Jenny Smith, Moira Hughes, Rita Borrow, Beck Simpson, Susan Gamble, Susan Poulson, Maisie King, Angela Fielding, Charlotte Needham. Councillors: –?–, –?–, Burton, Littlewood, Jane, Mrs Gell, Towel, Greenslade, Green, Salter, Sanders.

High jinks in Egerton Park at the Hospital Fête, June 1936. Daniel Hayes, fishmonger, of 33 Market Place is holding the donkey's head. Harold Pearce, gents outfitter, of 18 Market Place (Swan Porch) is behind the donkey organizing the rides, with Archie Sleath, sanitary inspector for the Rural District Council, cane at hand in case of trouble, on the extreme right of the photograph.

Leicestershire County Constabulary, Melton Mowbray Division, 1937. Back row, left to right: PCs Crowder, Smith, Pratt, Cliff, Humberston, Jasper, Webster. Middle row: PCs Goldstone, Blundy, Neale, Hewitt, Geary, Claxton, Baker, Jarvis, Topps, Bason. Front row: Sergeants Rickett, Meakin, Jones, Superintendent Gotheridge, Sergeants Hull, Bramall, Cave.

Melton Mowbray Fire Brigade, 1937. Back row, left to right: L. Haycox (inset), F. Stapleford, H. Beeken, F. Wood, G. Hack, C.E. Dawson, A.E. Rippon (inset). Front row: Capt F.G. Smith, H. Wallace, G.H. Newbold, D.A. Cunington.

Acknowledgements

The compilation of this book was only made possible by the help of many friends of the author. They have provided photographs and information without which this book could not have been published. Permission has been granted for all the photographs that are still in copyright. Should any person consider copyright material has been used without the holder's permission, the author offers his sincere apologies and will make an acknowledgement in future publications.

The basis of this collection of photographs is the author's own collection. The following people have provided help in many ways. The author's good friend Rigby Graham offered advice and provided the photographs of the goods yard in the town railway station, and excellent photographs recording the demolition of the Northern station. As usual, Nigel Moon gave good advice, and also provided the photograph of the bridge on Scalford Road and two other photographs. Margaret Portess provided many of the photographs and was able to assist in the compilation of many of the captions. Joe Ecob and Alan Richardson allowed the author access to their large collection of historic photographs; with their help the compilation of this book was made a lot easier.

Mr Peter Herrick, Borough Secretary and Clerk to the Melton Borough Council, gave the author permission to delve into the council archives; he was helped by Elaine Ferney, the tourism officer, and Marcia Coxhead. Many of the 'official' photographs came from this source. Bob Dove of the planning department provided the photograph of the crane on p. 89. Mrs S. Tindall provided the photographs on p. 131. Walter Robertson gave helpful advice on Royal families and provided the photographs on pp. 144 and 145. Jimmy Learmonth was extremely helpful as usual in providing information about and photographs of football teams in the Melton area. Ian Hickman provided a number of photographs covering cricket in the town. Gordon Williams, an 'Old Meltonian', was extremely helpful. He provided many photographs, but above all gave help and advice on compiling the captions.

Thanks are due to Mr and Mrs A. Charles for their professional help and for allowing the author permission to reproduce photographs from their collection. Christine Greaves, External Relations Administrator for Pedigree Petfoods, was most helpful and provided full permission to use photographs which are that company's copyright. No book of photographs depicting scenes of Melton Mowbray life would be complete without Stilton cheese and pork pies being included. The manufacturers of these products, Tuxford and Tebbutt, are part of the history of the town, and their factory manager, Mr A.M. Farquharson, provided an excellent collection of photographs for the author's use, without any restrictions being applied. Thanks are also due to the author's wife Pamela for tolerating a husband whose collecting habits tend to overshadow their household at times. Finally, thanks are due to Pat Peters for neatly typing the text for the publisher's use.

List of Places and Features
Part One: Around Melton Mowbray

Part Two: Melton Mowbray